THE PRIEST'S PRISONER

ROBERT K RYNIKER

The Priest's Prisoner

By

Robert K. Ryniker

STUDIO
OF BOOKS
THE SPACE FOR YOUR MESSAGE

Other Books by

Robert K. Ryniker

20 Years of Faith

The Trying Years

Sarah Shugar and the
Inheritance

Copyright © 2025 by Robert K. Ryniker

Studio of Books LLC
5900 Balcones Drive Suite 100
Austin, Texas 78731
www.studioofbooks.org
Hotline: (254) 800-1183

Ordering Information:
Special discounts are available on quantity purchases by corporations, associations, and others. For details, contact the publisher at the address above.

Printed in the United States of America.

ISBN-13: Softcover   978-1-964928-61-6
          eBook   978-1-964928-62-3
          Hardback

Dedication

This book is dedicated to our veterans, and those who died to preserve our freedom.

Introduction

In this story I followed through with the times, as they were many years ago, as I did in my first novel, Sarah Shugar and the Inheritance. In that book I wrote of the times as they would have been 138 years ago. This story is more recent, though it is still about a page of American history before most people living today were born.

Some of your parents may have told you about the way the world was during World War II, the greatest conflict in history. Although World War I (the war to end all wars) included many nations from Europe, parts of Asia, and North America, no war in history had so many nations in the world involved as the ones who fought on one side or another, than World War II. This story is not like the hundreds of many other books written about the coming of the war as it slowly began in Europe and eastern Asia, or the many battles fought until the war was finally brought to an end. The battles that were fought were necessary to end the war, but battles of a different kind were also fought on the home fronts of all the nations. For a while the people of Britain inspired people of the free world as they stood in defiance of a very strong Germany, with sacrifices given by the military, and the citizens as well, until the bombing of Pearl Harbor brought the United States into the war. From then on the United States could openly assist in sending much needed supplies to Britain, and also troops to insure the safety of Britain, and troops to fight the Germans in north Africa, before sending the navy to retake the many islands in the South Pacific that had been taken over by Japan, until the Philippines were retaken, and the final steps were underway to insure the final surrender of Japan.

But like the British citizens, who sacrificed in many ways before Pearl Harbor, American citizens also had to suddenly change their way of living in many ways. The rationing of gasoline, and other items, was necessary, as many industries were made to change to support our war effort. The auto makers in Detroit, and other places, had to change their machines to produce jeeps, tanks, planes, ammunition, & other things for the battles that our armies and naval forces would need. And, with millions of men going off to war, it was necessary for women to step up to fill many of the jobs the men had previously held, as the war icon "Rosie the Riveter" became symbolic of the work force that we had during the war, on the home front. And, as many of the women were mothers, necessary changes had to be made at home for the care of children.

You won't read much about the war battles in this story, but I think it is of great Importance to know how things were for the women, children, and older people who stayed at home and did their part to support our fighting men, chaplains, and medical personnel who were there to save many lives. The Church had to adapt, as many male parishioners were gone to war, and deal with the sorrow that came, when a loved one was sent home badly injured, killed in battle, or sometimes only becoming a memory, as a family was informed that their son was a prisoner of war, or missing in action.

I make more references to real history than in my Sarah Shugar book, where I mentioned only a few sketches of history. This book may bring back memories of some things learned in history class, or of things our parents passed on to us. But not many books about the World War II years were about the way things were at home, and very few books have been written about the part of our nation that I'm writing about. It includes what priests and other religious had to deal with at a time when, as a citizen, they had to support the war effort, which resulted in many men and women being killed, while still leading the people in the Faith they were all supposed to keep, even as God's children were killing each other, on a scale never before seen on this earth.

Table of Contents

About the Author

Travel back in time to the 1940s, when the people living in the United States' of State of Michigan. Explore what life was like for the residents of different states, as they navigated the World War II era. Gain insights into the way families lived during that period, a time when the world was grappling with the challenges of World War II. Robert K. Ryniker was born on November 13th, 1945, in Elmira, N. Y., The only child of Harry and Jean Ryniker. He attended Elmira schools and eventually enrolled at Elmira College, where he contributed weekly articles to the college newspaper, covering topics like hockey and other sports programs during his Junior and Senior years. Robert had previously authored two nonfiction books and made the decision in 2018 to embark on his first novel-writing journey.

Chapter 1

"Well, I still don't understand how he can put away that much food," said Marie Wicks, the cook and housekeeper for the Good Shepherd Church rectory. "I swear, you would think Father Salva was starved, but he usually tells me of the good lunch he had on his way to us for his two day stay, to give you a two day rest from your duties at Good Shepherd." "Well, it's just the way he is," said Father James O'Connell, pastor of Good Shepherd. "But even when Father Salva is here you still say a funeral Mass on Friday, or Saturday, even though you're supposed to have those days off for resting and praying," said Mrs. Wicks, a widow who came to work at the rectory 4 years previously, before Father Jim was made the new pastor by the Bishop of the Marquette Diocese. "You forget," said Father Jim, "that I've made promises to families that I would say the funeral Mass, or service, for when their loved one is called to their final reward." "I'm sorry, I forgot," said Marie.

"I'll get back to washing the windows," said Marie. Then, as she looked through the glass she said, "Why, Mr. Ansara is coming up the walk." "Yes," said Father O'Connell, "I have an appointment with him about his child's Confirmation." "Let's see," said Marie, "the oldest is 16 year old Caleb. Wasn't he Confirmed two years ago? Their 14 year old Elaine is next, right?" "Yes," said the pastor of Good Shepherd. "After her will be 11-year-old Linda, then 10 year old Billy, then 8 year old Adam," said Father Jim. "It still amazes me how you can remember the names and ages of our parish's children," said Mrs. Wicks. "Well, I can't remember all of them," said Father Jim. "After all, we've almost 100 families in the Parish; sometimes I have to drop a hint to get the parents to tell me their child's name."

So Father O'Connell answered the knock in the door and welcomed his friend Michael Ansara in, going with him to discuss the last instructions that would be given to Elaine, before her Confirmation. Marie finished cleaning the windows of the rectory before meeting with Michael Ansara as he was leaving the rectory.

"So, how's Jean?" asked Marie. "Oh, she's as happy as a wife could be, considering she's got me for a husband," said Michael. "Why, Michael, you know she's happy to have you, and your five children," said Marie. "I'm just so happy that Good Shepherd was built here five years ago. It was hard for me to take my wife and young children all the way to St. John's for Mass. In the snowy winter days, we sometimes couldn't make it there for 2 or 3 weeks," said Mike Ansara. "Yes,' said Marie, "I was told by the first housekeeper that you & the missus always felt it necessary to go to confession because you missed those weeks, but it wasn't really necessary." "Well, we don't miss Mass anymore, unless we have a real blizzard, where everything is shut down," said Michael. "Yes, I remember, it happened the first year I was here," said Marie. "All the churches, and business were closed, it took us two days to dig ourselves out."

It was almost five o'clock when Father Domino drove in the driveway, and came in the front door of the rectory. He was always there on Thursday for his two day visit, an hour or so before supper time. Marie said she could set the kitchen clock by his arrival. He was the part time pastor for St. John the Baptist Church in the eastern part of the Upper Peninsula of Michigan. The church was located at 420 Pine Street in Heeawatha, Michigan. It was the only Catholic Church besides the Marquette, until the Bishop realized that more Catholics were coming from the western part of the peninsula to get to Mass.

So, special funds were set aside to purchase two lots on Crescent Avenue for the building of a church, with the rectory at 359 Crescent Avenue, with the people in this part of the peninsula now having a church to go to. But it cut the number of families that went to St. John's to about 60, so they set things up for the St. John's pastor to say just a Mass on Sunday, with a daily Mass on Wednesday. The other days were for various church work, except for when the pastor went to Good Shepherd on Thursday, to say the daily Mass on Friday, and taking care of other church duties, before going back to St. John's Saturday afternoon to prepare for Sunday Mass the next morning.

"Hi. Marie!" said Father Domino. "Hello, father, you're right on time," said Marie. "Before you ask, we'll be having beef stew for supper, it's one of Father Jim's favorites. I made biscuits, will you be wanting seconds, again?" "Well, not of the biscuits, but probably seconds, maybe thirds, of the stew," said Father Salva. "Of course, why should this meal be any different than any other," mumbled Marie to herself. "What's that?" asked Father Salva. "Ohhh, nothing, I was just thinking of what I'll be having for tomorrow night," said Marie, as she made the sign of the cross.

Just then Father O'Connell came in the room, and said some private prayers, before coming to get ready for supper. "Hi, Jim," said Father Salva, as Father O'Connell finished his final prayer. "Hi, Salva," said Father Jim, "what's going on at St. John's?" "Well, I was a little busier this week. Sunday afternoon one of my oldest parishioners died," said Father Salva, the family called me to give him last rites. I was busy for the rest of the day with the family. I held his wake Monday night, then had a funeral Mass on Tuesday morning. There must have been 50 or more there for the Mass, more than usual for my funerals. So, with my Wednesday morning Mass, I've been a little busier than usual." "I've been busy all week," said Father Jim, "making sure that the final instructions will be completed by next week, for our five children who will be confirmed. I know it's the second week of August, I am making sure we can do the confirmation by the last week of August, before school starts. We'll probably have the Auxiliary Bishop for it. The Bishop has only been here once since I came here four years ago."

"Supper will be ready in 40 minutes," said Marie, as she went around the kitchen fixing things, in its turn. "While we wait," said Father Salva, "can I ask you a favor?" "What," said Father Jim. "Well, I'm afraid I might need a bit more gas, to get back to St. John's Saturday. With the funeral, I had to go and drive some people around who had used up their gas rations when they came from out of town," said Father Salva. "Yes, it's hard for some since the government had to limit gas for public use, along with sugar and other things because of the need to support our military, since the Japanese bombing of Pearl Harbor," said Father Jim. "I still have one ration left, but I might need it this weekend, I can't get any more rations until Monday or Tuesday." "At the least, it's good they give some more rations for gas to churches," said Father Salva. "Yes, it's because we might need more gas to get to someone's house out of town, or to a hospital," said Father Jim. "But I only have, maybe, about a quarter of a tank of gas," said Father Salva. "It takes about that much, sometimes more, to get from Cross Bear to Heeawatha." "Well, I may need the one coupon I have, so I'll siphon out about a gallon of gas from my car to your gas tank," said Father Jim. "That should be enough to get you home." "Thank you, I'll say a rosary for you," said Father Salva. "This way," said Father Jim, "I will still have my last coupon to get gas with, if I run out."

Soon supper was ready, and Father Salva lived up to his reputation for eating, as he put a little more stew in his bowl, after two full helpings. "I've baked an apple pie," said Marie, to Father Salva, maybe you would like some later." "Oh no, I still have some room for a piece now," said Father Salva. As Father Salva held out his plate Marie just shook her head as she gave him a piece of pie. "I still swear," whispered Marie to Fr. Jim, "I still can't see where he puts it."

After supper Father Jim and Father Salva went into the living room to listen to the radio. After washing the dishes quickly, Marie came in to join the two priests. "Oh, is the President on tonight?" asked Marie, "I do so much like his fireside chats, that started way back from before we were in the war. To me it seems like he is right there in the room with us, like a family member." "Yes," said Father Jim, "but to me the most inspirational one was the one told to the nation, the day after Pearl Harbor, when he asked Congress to declare that we are at war with Japan." "I liked the part where he said that we would win the inevitable outcome, so help us God," said Marie. Father Jim nodded, he liked the fact that we had a good Christian president, even if he wasn't a Catholic, and Father Salva said, "Yes, our God will deliver us."

Friday morning Father Salva said the 8 A. M. daily Mass, while Father Jim slept in until about 8 A. M., then read his Bible for about 20 minutes, as he got dressed and came downstairs to join Marie & Father Salva, as he was just returning from the church. As usual, Father Salva had seconds of eggs, toast, home fries, and coffee. Father Jim gave Father Salva a list of some of the parishioners who would be coming, for spiritual advice, in addition to his usual hearing of confessions from 11:00 until noon. Father Jim took advantage of his day off to call the mayor, and another church friend, to see if they wanted to go fishing with him. Robert Horton, the mayor of Cross Bear, said he would join him, but the other friend, Charlie Hayes, said that he had an errand to run, but that he would join him in about an hour. This was one way Father Jim had of keeping in touch with what was going on in the community, as well as enjoying a day of fishing, often for his supper.

About an hour later, after Father Jim and Robert Horton were there, fishing in the creek, Charlie Hayes joined them. Father Jim had already, in his basket, a good sized trout, and a sunfish. The mayor had just one small sunfish. "It isn't fair," said the mayor, Father has help upstairs." Charles Hayes had his 12 year old son Cody with him, he liked to fish, too. "What about

Hank?" said Father Jim, referring to another of Charles' sons. "Oh, he got behind in his chores, I made him stay home until they were done," said Charles. "He might join us, later." "What about your girl, Lisa?" said the mayor, "I thought she liked to fish, also." "Oh, she was busy helping her mother with cleaning, and she had to stay and watch her 4 year old brother Francis, while her mother went to visit someone," said Charles. "That Lisa, even though she's 8, has her way with her 12 and 9 year old brothers, doesn't she?" said the mayor. "Yes," said Charles, "they each tried to push her around once, but she used all her wiry strength as she fought them off. She rules the roost, now. She's a good girl, but no one takes advantage of her, her teacher told me that." "You mean Louise Drucker? She rules the kids in a very strict way. Maybe Lisa takes after her," said the mayor. "Maybe," said Charles. "But she's very good to her 4 year old Francis, she's like a second mother to him sometimes." "Well, it looks like everybody knows their place in the family," said the mayor. "Like a chicken in a barnyard," said Charles, "they have a pecking order. But I bet Lisa won't ever let anyone "peck" on her brother Francis."

"Oh, I think you've got another one," said Charles to Father Jim. Father did, indeed have something, as he pulled in a nice bass. "We'll have fish for supper tonight," said Father Jim. "I still say you have pull, upstairs," said the mayor, as he pointed to the sky. Father Jim just said nothing, and shrugged, in innocence. "Oh, by the way," said Father Jim to Charles, "Pete Nolan had to go out of town to help his sick mother, he won't be here for Sunday Mass. Can you take his place for taking up the collection?" "Why sure," said Charles, "Oh, will I get the same "cut" from the collection as Pete gets?" "Of course," said Father Jim. "It's a nice, round number." Charles smiled, he knew what Father meant.

After Father Jim came back to the rectory with some nice fish, Marie was able to fix a nice fish dinner for Father Jim and Father Salva, enough for Father Salva to have seconds, as usual, as he said to Marie, I prefer the trout, if there's enough." Later

Father Jim and Father Salva, and Marie, relaxed in the living room, as they listened to the radio. Then Father Salva said to Father Jim, Marie says you remember all the kid's names in the parish, is that right?" "Well, not really. I remember most of them, not quite all," said Father Jim. "It's wonderful to have a memory as good as that," said Father Salva. "I can't remember what I had for supper yesterday." "Beef stew, two and a half helpings," said Marie. "Very good," said Father Salva. "But with towns, and streets, I only remember that my town is an Indian name, and the street St. John's is on is named because of all the pines on the street. I do know that Cross Bear was named for a mean bear that was here, and was hard to kill. But your street, will you tell me again how it was named? I know you told me once." "We told you twice," said Marie. "As I said before," said Father Jim," more than 60 years ago people came from the lower part of Michigan, to settle in the Upper Peninsula, making towns out of little hamlets. When they made a town here, they named the streets in some strange ways. Since the street we are on was wider than the other streets. They decided to make it an avenue. A crescent moon was out that night, and since the road showed up, even with a crescent moon, they called it Crescent Avenue."

Marie finished reading the two passages from the Bible that she read each night, and said goodnight to Father Jim and Father Salva, then went upstairs to bed. Father Jim and Father Salva then talked for about an hour about stories that had been passed on from Europe about how Hitler was imprisoning many Jews, and some other people, including Catholics, and how Pope Pius XII was in a bad situation, since he was wary of what Germany might do to some people, while still trying to keep his moral position as the leader of the Catholic Church, and its people. Although the details were not proven, they both realized that at least some of what they heard was true. So, they both went up to bed agreeing that thy would say some extra prayers for the Pope, and for the injustices being done to God's people.

The next morning, after breakfast, Father Jim went again to his usual spot at Ottawa Creek to spend another day off, fishing. Father Salva heard confessions from 9:30 to 11:30, with Stations of the Cross right after confessions. Then he went to the rectory for lunch. Marie had made a lunch for Father Jim to eat while he was fishing.

Today the mayor was busy with a town meeting, but his friend Charles Hayes was there to join Father Jim again, along with his three oldest children, 12 year old Cody, who was there yesterday, and also his 9 year old brother Hank, and 8 year old sister Lisa. Charlie's wife, Emma, had stayed home with 4 year old Francis. "So," said Father Jim, "who's the best fisherman in the family?" "Daddy is," said Lisa. "No, I am the best," said Cody. "Well, let's just see how we do today," said Father Jim, to keep the peace. Charles nodded to Father, he didn't want a family squabble there, while they were fishing. So, they had a good morning, and afternoon fishing together, as Father Jim answered many questions from Charles' three children, about the priesthood and about God, as well as why he likes being a priest. Charles also asked a question about the situation in Europe, which Father was unable to give a complete answer to, because of the limited reliable sources from the European theater, at this point.

When they all left about 5 o'clock, Father Jim had 4 fish. Lisa did the best in her family with 4 fish, with her father and 9 year old brother catching 3, and with her 12 year old brother, who had claimed to be the best fisherman, with only 2 fish. But the Hayes family had enough for a good fish dinner. Four year old Francis said he wanted to go fishing, too. His father told him he would get him a pole so he could go with them on their next trip. He knew that his sons and daughter would be happy to show him how to fish.

That evening Marie cleaned the fish Father had caught, and put them in the freezer part of the icebox, to have some other time. Marie had cooked a nice chicken dinner for Father Jim, and for Father Salva, who had decided to stay until supper, before going back to St. John's. After his usual seconds, Father Salva left for home, so that he could get back in time to prepare for Sunday Mass the next morning.

On Sunday Father Jim rose early, to get to church on time to turn on the lights, and say a rosary before getting the chalice and other things out for the altar boys to take care of when they came. One of the older of Father Jim's parishioners was there when Father came, with a prayer book as he said a rosary. The church was always open for anyone who wanted to make a visit, say some prayers, or light a votive candle. Father greeted him, he was Will Geer, a long time parishioner who knew the Bible better than most of the parishioners. He was a gardener. Father knew that his beloved wife, Ellen Corby Geer, would be along soon, with other family members.

Mass starts at 9 A. M. it was already after 8:30 when the two altar boys for this week came in, with their families following. 16 year old Caleb Ansara and 12 year old Cody Hayes were scheduled this week, and they went right to work, putting on their white albs, and doing what Father Jim told them to get things ready on the altar, and with putting the Lectionary on the pulpit. By 8:50 the candles were lit on the altar, everything was set for the faithful parishioners, most of whom were there already, as most of the people got there at least a few minutes early for Mass. Only 4 or 5 came in a couple of minutes late, about the time Father was starting the Mass with the opening prayer.

The Mass went smoothly, as usual, with Father giving a homily on the Good Samaritan, and tied it in with the sad fact that the men at war could not treat each other as the Good Samaritan did. Father's fishing friend, Charles, father of the altar boy Cody Hayes, did take Pete Nolan's place for taking up the collection. One of the other ushers took the bag of money up to the front of the church, where Father Jim would get it after Mass. Less than half of the people came up for Communion, not as many as for last Sunday. About half of the choir sang the recessional verse. Father Jim wished he could have more of the 11 singers for every Sunday, instead of just for Christmas. He would try to work on that for next Sunday.

Father greeted his people, as always, as they left the church. As one woman told Father she was in a family way, another family asked for a visit to their house to talk to a sick family member. Father stopped 3 of the parents who had a child who was going to be confirmed, to make sure the child knew when to come for their final instructions this week. Many told Father about what they liked about his homily, especially the part where Father had told of their many young men who were about to go overseas to fight for their nation. Meanwhile the altar boys were doing their job as they snuffed out the candles on the altar, put the chalice and Lectionary away in the sacristy, took off their albs and hung them up neatly for next week's altar boys. They then waited for Father Jim to come to see it Father had anything more for them to do. But Fr. Jim told them that he would check the votive candles himself, so they could go. He thanked them as they left, and they thanked him for letting them serve, as 12 year old Cody said he thinks he wants to be a priest someday.

Upon getting back to the rectory, Father Jim saw that Marie had their breakfast almost ready. They always had late breakfast on Sunday, at around 10:30 or later, after Mass, since they had to fast from midnight on if they were going to receive Holy Communion. Father Jim was surprised to see that Marie was serving bacon, along with the eggs and toast. A parishioner had dropped some off yesterday to help in supporting their church. Marie told Father it was from John Gannor, who raised pigs, along with a ham to cook later on. "Yes, he's fortunate to have good food," said Father Jim. "Many of our parishioners were just getting by before the war started for us, but now it's harder for some to get along, with rationing, and the scarceness of some foods, and consumer goods that we took for granted before much of our industrial output was set up to produce weapons, and other things needed for the war. Some people help themselves out by hunting, fishing, and growing their own gardens. But many still don't have enough money to buy the food they need, especially if a family has children." "Yes," said Marie, "and here's some, like the Talbot family, eight children to feed, seven of them girls. Only the last one was a boy. He's what, about 2 years old?" "Almost," said Father Jim. "And the oldest one, Alice, will be 13 soon. Only one family in the parish has more children that the Talbots. We must do something here to raise some money for our poor parishioners." "But what can we do?" asked Marie. "Well, other churches, or clubs, do things to raise money. Some have a place where they put on a show of some kind, and charge admission to see the show. Others have sold things they don't want anymore, or have a bake sale, or pancake breakfast," said Father Jim. "I heard that some churches in the southern part of Michigan have bingos," said Marie. "Yes, but you have to have a place big enough for tables and chairs, and other things for running a bingo," said Father Jim. "It takes some money just to get started, with people who have money to spend. If our people had the money they would use it for the food they need, and other incidentals, like clothes." "Are you, now, thinking of having something to raise money for our needy?" asked Marie. "Yes, some of our parishioners have some money to spend, but we must think of a way to give to our needy," said Father Jim, "like a prize, book, or something of that sort. The ones who would gladly give are the ones who need help." "Well, let's sleep on it, said Marie. "I'll try to get an idea from my fishing friends tomorrow," said Father Jim. Good night, Marie, I'll see you in the morning." "I'll get to church first, to say my rosary for an answer to helping those in need," said Marie.

Chapter 2

The 3rd week of August, 1942, went by fast at Good Shepherd, with 4 of the 5 candidates for Confirmation finishing up with their last studies, as the 5th candidate, who lived several miles out of town, was receiving private tutoring. The arrangements were made, through the Bishop, for a Confirmation class on Saturday evening. The Bishop would remain overnight, and preside at the Sunday morning Mass. As Father Jim expected, the Auxiliary Bishop Rev. Christopher P. O'Hanlon, O.P., would be coming, in place of the Bishop.

The church had to be decorated for the event, as several parishioners would be providing roses and other home grown flowers for the church, with some others putting up paper banners, like the ones used for church for Christmas or Easter. Some women of the parish would see that the hardwood floors were clean, and that all the windows of the church would be sparkling, and especially the round, stained – glass window at the front of the church, behind the altar. When the church was built, there was only enough money for one stained glass window, because of the money that was spent on a good altar, and pews made out of prime mahogany.

But, aside from his regular pastoral duties, Father Jim spent most of his spare time getting something done for a fundraiser. First he paid a visit to Mayor Robert Horton, to let him know what he was planning, and to get some help from others in town, through the church. He met with his fishing friend Charles Hayes, Michael Ansara, Clint Walker, Rowley Yates, Barnaby West, and

Ellen Alda, and their families. Ellen was a seamstress, and said she had some extra clothing and blankets that she would offer for prizes, or for selling. She also talked to other women, and their husbands, who said that they would also look for things they could spare from their house, barn, or other places, to donate for the fundraiser. A meeting was held with those who showed an interest, in the rectory. They finally agreed to hold a sale of all items that could get, along with baked goods and other cooked food for sale to all attending. John Gannor said he would donate 2 hams and a side of bacon for the meals, and Fess Barker said he would hunt some animals, from rabbits, to deer, to give for selling. Lorne Green said he would offer a steer from his herd for the fundraiser, and Dale Roberts said he would offer his horses and wagon for transportation, for anyone who needed help for getting to the fundraiser. Richard Barkley said he would offer a steer for selling, and Colleen Bowman, who was a nurse, offered her services, in case of an emergency, or accident, along with Doctor Milburn Stone. Waitress Phyllis Thaxter said that she would help with the serving and cooking of the meals. And Doug McClure also said he would offer a steer to sell.

Most of the rest of the parishioners didn't have anything to give worth selling, but all said they would help out wherever needed, and that they would spread the word about their endeavor outside the church. After much discussion, they decided to hold the fundraiser on the church grounds, on Friday after-noon and evening, and again on Saturday, from 8 AM to 4:30 PM. They would be closing up just before the Bishop would be presiding for their Confirmation. Father Jim said that different families had different needs, so that afterward they would have the families come to the rectory, where it would be decided how much of the money raised could be given to them. At the last meeting Father Jim said, "It would be nice if we could raise $400. Then we could afford to give at least $10 to each needy person, and more, depending on their needs, and family size. At least 60 of our families are in some need. We can ask our parishioners not to come for help if they don't need it, so that the ones who really need it will get more."

So, each day different parishioners came to Good Shepherd Church to report on how things were going on one thing or another. A member of the parish, Marjorie Mane, was a secretary, so she typed up notices about the 2 day sale at the church, which members of the parish hung up at some stores, and passed out to other people.

On Sunday Father Jim had the mayor give a report on their progress, with many thanks given for those who were giving of their time and talents. Items for sale were piling up in the church basement, and in the rectory. A letter was sent to the Auxiliary Bishop about it, so that he wouldn't wonder what was going on, when he got there on Saturday, for the Confirmation. The bishop even wrote back and said that he would look at the items they had for sale, and that he would probably buy something to help with their fundraiser. The Ansara and Hayes families both took part in the preparations, and also the Arness family, which was a younger family. They had been married for 5 years, and had a 4 year old daughter Mary, and a 2 year old son James. Jean Arness was also in a family way again. Many families had their children help out, while some older members of the family busied themselves with knitting, or chair making, or other things for selling. Some of the women would do the cooking. The hams that were donated would be good for a nice ham dinner for Saturday. Fish dinners would be served for the Friday meal. All this activity did more than prepare for the fundraiser. It also brought the church members together for a common cause. People who had not seen each other for a while brought each other up to date on their own families, and the good feelings of doing something for God's neediest children. as well as, unfortunately, talk about the war. Parents told friends about their sons who were in the military, and, in some cases, where they were stationed. Some mothers showed others a letter they had received, which would in every case, be treasured, and be treasured even more in the future if their son was one of the many soldiers who never returned home.

But, in spite of all the preparations for the fundraiser, regular church activities went on, with the Monday through Friday daily Masses, regular meetings with Father Jim about personal and spiritual matters confessions, and of course the last meetings with the five children who would be Confirmed on the second day of the fundraiser.

"Oh, I don't know if I can keep up with this," said Marie, in reference to answering the door all day to let people in to see Father Jim about the progress so far, or for another matter. "Well, it's Wednesday, in a few days it will all be over," said Father Jim. "And with all your duties at the rectory, you're still doing some baking for the bake sale," said Father Jim to Marie. "I'll do most of it Thursday night, and Friday morning," said Marie, "so that all my pies and cakes will be fresh. And, of course, I'll have the usual larger meal to fix on Thursday, when the human stomach gets here." "That's not a nice way to refer to a man of the cloth," said Father Jim. "Well, you know what I mean," said Marie. "I'll bet his mother did not give him seconds and thirds at the table when he was growing up." "Well, I don't know about that, but be glad you're not feeding him all week long," said Father Jim. "I guess I can be thankful for small favors," said Marie, It was two minutes before 5 PM, on Thursday, one day before the fundraiser, when Marie looked out the window to see Father Salva driving his old 1934 Chevrolet into the driveway. "Right on time," said Marie, as she told of Father Salva's arrival. "I'm going to make sure he stays away from the cookies, brownies, and the other things I'm baking for the bake sale tomorrow." "Oh, I think they'll be safe," said Father Jim. He knows about our fundraiser, and that you are doing things for the bake sale." "I'm still going to remind him what my baking is for," said Marie.

The supper was good, as Marie had fixed roast chicken, with potatoes, and peas. Marie noticed it when Father Salva looked over at the trays of cookies, brownies, and 2 apple pies. But one of the apple pies was for their dessert, so Father Salva was delighted to have a second piece of pie.

After supper a few more parishioners came to report on what they were doing for the fundraiser, as Father Jim told them where to put things, so they would be there on hand to start the fundraiser, at 1 PM, just after lunch.

They had a quick breakfast Friday morning, after Father Salva came back from saying morning Mass. Then parishioners started coming to set up tables, chairs, and other things for sale, including 4 steers donated by ranchers. Ladies were starting to bring pies, cakes, cookies, and other baked goods, along with some fruits and vegetables that some of the parishioners had in their gardens and orchards. Knitted goods were also brought, and crafts of all kinds, all priced lower than they would be in a store. Some chickens, ducks, and hogs were also donated. Fish were there that had been caught by a dozen or more fishermen on Wednesday and Thursday to be cooked for a nice fish dinner later on, which would cost $1.25, including potatoes, a vegetable, and a glass of lemonade or apple juice. For 20 cents more they could have a piece of apple or cherry pie, or a piece of cake. Each table had a money box for putting the cash in for the meal, or for other things purchased, with a person designated to receive the money & to keep an eye on the cash at all times, since someone might be tempted to take some money, as there was no way of accounting for the amount, aside from the dollars and change they started with, in order to give people change. Father Jim and the mayor would go around and collect some money every hour or so, as they put the money into bags with a piece of paper in it to keep track later on of how much they made from each table.

At 1 o'clock customers were already there, about half of them parishioners from the church, as they looked over the items on the tables, while some others started looking over the livestock for sale, as well as the produce brought in that morning. Others looked at the crafts and baked goods, while others started taking part in some of the games, where a person could win a small prize, or some item donated by some of the town merchants.

A lot of people there were strangers, not members of Good Shepherd. They were there because of the food, festivities, or items they could win in a balloon game, or a card game that was set up for giving small prizes. Word of the steers & other animals to buy at below market price had spread, and by 2 o'clock 2 of the steers had been sold, for $25 each, about $8 below the market price. Two of the hams were also sold for $5 each, about $2 below the market price. Father Jim was walking around seeing that things were going on as planned, and to visit with others, some of whom were parishioners with news about their families, as they discussed about how many people were there, and about how nicely things were set up, and organized in a very professional manner.

"I saw Father Salva," said Marie to Father Jim. "He bought two boxes of the cookies, and a glass of lemonade. And, five minutes later they were gone. Then he went to buy two boxes of fudge. Well, maybe he won't eat as much at our supper tonight," said Father Jim. "We're not having our supper at the rectory tonight," said Marie, "Everyone will be having a fish dinner here. Each person will have a choice of bass, trout, sunfish, or carp, with potato or macaroni salad, bread, and a drink, with cake or pie for dessert, for $1.25. Since the fish were all caught by about 15 people who caught them, mostly children, our only cost is for the salad, bread, drink, and dessert." "Yes," said Father Jim, it cost about $16 for the other things, but after about 14 people, the rest will be profit."

The rest of the first day went smoothly, and with 34 people having a nice fish dinner, a good profit was made. Father Salva, of course, bought 2 fish dinners, and paid for them, even though the ladies doing the cooking offered to give him a free dinner.

Then those whose job it was to do the cleaning up started doing their job at 8 o'clock, and were finished by 9, when everyone went home to rest up in preparation for coming back to do their jobs at 9 AM Saturday morning.

Everything went along easier on Saturday, since the people were used to doing their job now. Some who couldn't get away from their job, or their farm, on Friday, came on Saturday. And were showed how to help with things. The Bishop got there in the early afternoon, after coming from the parish rectory. After being introduced to some parishioners who hadn't met him, Father Jim Showed the Aux. Bishop around, showing him what they were selling, and the other things they had going on for raising money for their needy parishioners. The Auxiliary Bishop started helping their cause by buying some cookies, some brownies, and a pie for bringing back to the Bishop, who had given him $10.00 of his own money, to help out. Bishop O'Hanlon also bought some crafts and some other items for himself, as he wrote down in a notepad everything that was going on so that he could give a report to the Bishop when he got back.

4:30 came quickly, and everyone did what they needed to do, closing up their table or other part of the fundraiser for now, with most of the Good Shepherd people getting ready to go to the special Confirmation Mass, which was scheduled for 5:45. The five candidates for Confirmation were dressed up in their Sunday best, and ready to take this important step in their Catholic life. The Auxiliary Bishop had his own robe, and Father Jim supplied the other items for the Mass.

At 5:45 the church was almost full, almost like on Sunday, with many of the family, and friends of the five candidates, there for the fine church celebration that was held at Good Shepherd every other year. A small group of singers sang the song Immaculate Mary as the procession came into the church, led by the Cross bearer, two altar boys with candles, the five candidates, Father Jim, and the Bishop. The families of the candidates were in the front pews of the church, along with the sponsors for each child. The Mass went along smoothly, as Father Jim gave the homily, where he told of each child as he knew him or her, and of the importance of Confirmation.

Then the Bishop did his part to confirm the children. Then Communion was held, with the Bishop giving out Communion on one side, and Father Jim giving out Communion on the other. Most of the people came up to receive, since the Bishop had announced that all who fasted for at least 3 hours before Mass could receive. The choir sang the song How Great Thou Art as the procession left the church, with five new Catholics, who were beaming, with the joy of being in full communion with the Church.

Supper was held at the rectory, as the Bishop looked on with amazement as Father Salva again had two helpings, and part of a third. "I'm so glad you cooked a lot" said Father Salva, "it's been more than 5 hours since I had something at the fundraiser." "Well, it's not as long as fasting from midnight until morning Mass," said Marie.

After supper Father Jim, Father Salva, and the Bishop talked about the special day it was here, with the second day of the fundraiser, followed by the Confirmation. "I'll have a good report to give to the Bishop," said the Auxiliary Bishop O'Hanlon. "I talked much with the five children after Mass, two of the boys said they want to be a priest when they grow up, and one of the 2 girls said she wants to become a nun." "I know which ones you mean," said Father Jim. The boys are 14 year old Robert West and 13 year old Henry Tucker, and the girl is 14 year old Elaine Ansara." "You really do know your parishioners," said the Bishop. "I'll include that in my report to His Eminence. I'll also see if there's anything more the Diocese can do to help in this time of shortages, since the war has changed our lives in so many ways."

After a well – deserved night's rest Father Jim got up Sunday morning and made the church was set up. More parishioners were there than usual because of the Bishop was there to celebrate the Mass, as Father Jim acted as the concelebrant. Bishop O'Hanlon gave the homily, as he told of some of the things that were going on in the Diocese, and the latest word from Pope Pius XII. He congratulated Father O'Connell, & the people of Good Shepherd Church for their successful fundraiser for the needy, and congratulated the 5 new Confirmants. Finally, he thanked everyone here for welcoming him, and treating him so well; he would have a good report to give to the Bishop when he returned. Father Jim also said a few words, as he thanked the Bishop for coming, and a final thanks to the parishioners for their help in raising some money for their own faithful in need of the church's help.

After Mass Bishop O'Hanlon had breakfast at the rectory before taking two boxes of the cookies and other goods he had bought at the fundraiser. He even bought one of the three hams that were donated, for only $3, about two dollars less than the church in Marquette usually paid. About 1:30 he got into his late model 1940 Ford, and left for the home church, where he would once more make a trip back to Marquette to give his report to the Bishop.

Back at Good Shepherd the mayor and a staff of parishioners were at work putting the things away that were left over from the fundraiser, as well as tables and chairs. Then the task began of counting the money that was taken in, after repaying some of the people for costs involved in the meals that were made, which only came to less than $25. Everything else was all profit, since the ingredients for making the baked goods were all donated, as all the men and women gave of their time and work for the church. The best single money maker was the four donated steers, which sold for $25 each. The pig that was donated sold for $15, and almost all of the chickens that were donated sold for a total of $52. The cake booth brought in more than $90, and more than $180 was made for the meals, even after subtracting a little less than $21 for expenses. The games that people played brought in more than $100. When the final total was tallied, they made $529.35, about $120 more than Father Jim had hoped for. "We'll be able to give $10 to each of the 7 single people, and more to the 53 needy families," said Father Jim. "We will be able to give $15 to families with only one child, and $20 or more to families with 2 or more children, depending on their need, and the number of children. "Anything will be of help to those who are just getting by," said Marie. Father Jim said that they would figure it out on paper, and have their needy families come on Thursday to receive their amount, or on Friday, for those who couldn't make it on Thursday. This message was passed on to the needy families by church volunteers who lived near them personally, since most of the needy families didn't have a telephone.

Then, on Tuesday, the phone rang at the rectory. Marie answered it, and said, "Oh, it's Bishop O'Hanlon." So Father Jim took the phone, nodded his head a few times, said "I see" a couple of times, then thanked the Bishop very much. Marie looked eagerly at Father Jim for the news. "The Bishop just told me that, In support for our fundraiser, while Bishop O'Hanlon was here, the Bishop had a special collection taken up for our cause, at both of their Sunday Masses," said Father Jim. "They came up with a total of $117.72 to add to what we made. The Bishop put in the rest to make it an even $120. He said they would wire it to our bank account, so that we could give some more to the ones in need. That means we'll be able to give about $5 more to the neediest families, probably about $25, maybe $30 to the larger families." "That's wonderful!" said Marie. "I know the extra rosaries I said for the fund-raiser were heard. God does work in mysterious ways, as long as we call to Him. And trust in His word." "Yes," said Father Jim, "I said extra prayers, also. We must never have any doubt on the power of prayer." "Yes, we'll have to get to work re-figuring how much we'll be giving to the people," said Father Jim. "And we'll have to send a thank you note to the Bishop, and a separate one to Bishop O'Hanlon, also," said Marie.

Robert K. Ryniker

Later Marie said, "The Bishop was impressed with the way we were able to run our fundraiser, as well as the celebration of the Confirmation Mass." But Father Jim said, "We didn't have enough singers to make the songs sound good. We only had 11 singers, not much more than we usually have for a funeral Mass. And, with only 3 men there wasn't enough balance for songs sung in 4 parts; the eight women pretty much drowned out the men. "Sometime soon I'm going to try to get 3 or 4 more men for our choir, with maybe a few more women, also." "But, first," said Marie, "we must see to giving from the fruits of our labors, and prayers. We must do first things first."

Chapter 3

Everything was going good at Good Shepherd Church, as people who were the recipients of money from the fundraiser were now able to get some food, and some other things they needed. Some families who owed $5 or more at the general store were able to pay their bill, and buy some more items with cash, which helped both the ones who payed their bill, and the store owners, and the community, as a whole. But Father Jim was still thinking of getting more men for singing in the choir, so he put up signs in some stores that asked for more men to sing for the Lord. "I do not know how many men we will get," said Father Jim to Marie, "but they can't shoot me for trying."

One man came a day after the signs were put up, and asked to talk with Father Jim. "I sang with my family when I was a kid," said Frankie Lane, I think I could sing in the choir." So Father Jim brought out a church hymnal and had him sing a couple of songs. Father Jim said that he saw that he could read music, and that he had a good tenor voice; he would be welcome to join the choir. He told him that he would get in touch with him when he had some more men, so they could meet in the church for a rehearsal, for Mass.

The next day another man came, but he was not good at singing, or reading music, and Father Jim politely told him he would let him know if they needed him. "Why didn't you just tell him that he just isn't a singer?" said Marie. "Well, this way I won't hurt his feelings. And who knows, if he gets so he can read music, he might just be able to join the choir," said Father Jim. "But a sour note in the song would be worse than just an additional voice," said Marie. Father Jim nodded, he knew she was right.

In the next few days some other men came to volunteer for a part in the choir, but most were farmers, trappers, hunters, men who had never had any experience in singing in a choir, so Father Jim put them all "on hold," on a waiting list, in case they were really needed. He did find out that Terry Wilson, a farmer, was a singer, so he added him, and also Joan Blondell, a beautician, who asked if she could join the women. So Father Jim added her to the choir, also. "Well, we have five men now," said Father Jim, "but it still won't be a very good balance, with 5 men and 12 women."

The next day a man came to the rectory while Father Jim was in the church, leading with the stations of the Cross, after hearing confessions for two hours. Marie answered the door, and stepped back a step as she looked at the disheveled man in front of her. He had an unshaven face that was not very clean His hands and arms were also dirty, and his clothes were worn, and tattered in some places, with a few holes in his shirt, and one also in his pants. His shoes were also worn, and had seen better days. Marie stood there for a moment, wondering if she should say, or whether she should ask him to come in. Then the stranger spoke. "Hello, missus, my name is Hans Kruger. I saw the sign in a store with the name Father James O'Connell on it about you looking for men to sing in choir; I think I could help. I used to sing, and I'm Catholic, so I think I would do all right." "Oh, I'm sorry," said Marie. I was just startled, as you were a stranger." "You needn't pretend, missus," said the stranger, "I know I'm dirty, and with ragged clothes. I've been traveling across the hills, as I was just looking for work, and a place to stay." "Come in," said Marie, "have you eaten today?" "No, the last I ate was yesterday, when I came across an apple orchard.

I slept in a nearby shed last night, before coming into the town, where I saw the sign asking for men singers." "Well, Hans," said Marie, "you go to the washroom and clean your face and hands. I'll make you a late breakfast. Oh, my name is Marie."

As Hans Kruger washed Marie fixed a good breakfast with 2 eggs, toast, Some home fries, and coffee. Hans showed how hungry he was as he ate the food in front of him in about 10 minutes. Marie couldn't help but think of Fr. Salva as she watched Hans eat, but she knew that he hadn't eaten since the day before. "Are you all right?" asked Marie, "would you like some more?" "Oh," said Hans, "maybe just one more egg and slice of toast. But I don't have any money to pay for it." "Don't worry," said Marie, "this isn't a restaurant, we are always glad to help one of God's children." So Marie fixed 2 more eggs, for good measure, and a slice of toast for her nearly starved visitor. "Father Jim will be back from church soon," said Marie. "He's just finishing with Stations of the Cross, we usually have about 20 people there for that." "Oh, I haven't done the Stations of the Cross for a long time," said Hans. "I haven't been to Mass for a long time, either. I've been mostly in the country as I traveled from one place to another in the south part of the United States."

Just then Father Jim came in, after finishing with the Stations. He began to say something, but stopped short, as he saw a somewhat dirty stranger at the dinner table. Hans was just finishing his last egg, and drinking a sip of his coffee. "Father," said Marie, "he came to the door, offering to sing in our choir." "I'm Catholic," said the visitor. "His name is Hans" "Kruger," said the man as he took his last sip of coffee. "He hadn't eaten since yesterday, and just apples then," said Marie, "so I fixed him a late breakfast." "Well, that's good you could be here," said Father Jim, "so, you can sing?" "Yes, but I really need to find some work, so that I can pay for my keep, and for a place to stay," said Hans. "Well, I think you'll have a better chance of finding work if you finished cleaning up, and had some decent clothes to wear." said Father Jim "We have a bathtub you can use, and some clothes in a closet we give to anyone who needs them.

I'm sure you can find something that will fit you. We also have some shoes, I think the ones you have are about worn out." "I've been through creek beds and rough hills with them, on my way here," said Hans. "I don't really even know where I am. "You're in the town of Cross Bear, this is Good Shepherd Church, the western most part of the Marquette Diocese," said Father Jim. "You have a.... market diocese? asked Hans. "No, it's not market, it's Marquette," said Father Jim, as he spelled out the name. "The central city Marquette covers the entire Upper Peninsula of Michigan. It was named after a famous explorer who was in this part of the country, many years ago," said Father Jim. "You have a very nice church," said Hans, "I would like to attend Mass again. It's been a long time since I last went, more than a year ago. I can't receive communion because it's been a long time since I went to confession." "Tomorrow's Mass is at 8 AM," said Father Jim. "If you get there by 7:30 I'll hear your confession first." "But now," said Marie, "you go upstairs and get cleaned up and put some new clothes on. We also have some pajamas, you can sleep in the bed in the spare room." "Oh, thank you so much for everything," said Hans, I just wish I could repay you. I can work, doing just about anything. Do you have any jobs that need doing at the church? I can do carpentry work, do some mechanical work, chop wood, do lots of things," said Hans. "Well, I don't think we have any work here, and now," said Father Jim, but once you're cleaned up and in new clothes we can see what is available in the town. "I can check with the mayor and with Michael Ansara, one of our parishioners, sometimes he has work, or might know of someone who could give you a job. But for now take care of yourself, get a good night's sleep, you can use my razor if you want to shave." "Thank you, I'll do that," said Hans. "I would feel better cleaned up, and shaved." "My razor and shaving cream are in the cabinet on the wall in the wash room," said Father Jim. "I'll find them," said Hans.

In the morning Hans came down the stairs with a new clean shirt and a pair of nice pants, and a used, but decent shoes. Marie met him, and could hardly believe that this clean, shaven, neatly dressed man was the same man she had met at the door yesterday. "Why, you look very nice," said Marie to Hans. "Yes, and I thank you all for everything, especially for a real bed to sleep in, it's the first bed I've slept in since about 6 weeks ago," missus Marie." said Hans. "You can just call me Marie, everyone else does," said Marie. "Father Jim just left for the church, he said you would be meeting him for confession." "Oh yes, I'd better get going, but could I have a slice of toast and a drink of coffee, first?" said Hans. "Not if you intend on receiving communion," said Marie. "Oh, I haven't received for so long, I forgot about fasting. I have to wait, how many hours?" asked Hans. "From midnight on," said Marie. "Oh yes, I guess I forgot," said Hans. "How can I find the confessional?" "Just turn to your left, after you come in the front," said Marie. Hans nodded, and left the rectory for the front of the church.

Hans Kruger entered the church, and was awed by the beauty of the 1st church he had seen from the inside, for a long time. He looked at the beautiful stained glass window, the nice mahogany pews, and the Stations of the Cross. He felt a peace that comes to a person when they enter the House of the Lord. Then he looked for the confessional, and went to it, as he saw Father Jim's two feet below the curtain, and went into the door on the side to say his first confession in more than a year. Father Jim expected Hans' confession to be a long one, but it only took a few minutes for Hans to confess that he had missed Mass many times, that he had been angry with some people, and that he had used the Lord's name in vain a few times. Father Jim absolved him of his sins, and gave him a light penance – 3 Hail Marys. Then Father Jim said, "Come up to the front of the church, several people are already there for the Mass. One of the men that I told you about for a possible job is now walking in." "Mike," said Father Jim to his old friend, "this is a friend, Hans Kruger. He's been down on his luck, and traveled for many miles across the country to join us here, and to sing in our choir. But he is in need of a place to stay, and a job. He came to us when he saw a poster asking for men singers. Do you know of anyone who could use him for work, at least for now? He's been away from the church for a while, but he's back now. I'll vouch for him, I'm letting him stay at the rectory for now." "Well," said Michael, "remember how last week I just finished putting that new room in my store? I have some more new goods coming in, and I need to move some of the goods from the main room to the new room, and some new things I have, and other I will be getting, into the main room. I'm getting some consumer goods that are hard to find now, and I have several people waiting to buy them, when I have them in the store. The wife helps out some, with waiting on customers, but with the kids back in school now, she's pretty busy with other things, like her gardening and canning. I can use…" "Hans Kruber is his name," said Father Jim. "I can use you, Hans, if you can move the stock where I want it, while I wait on customers and keep the store running" said Michael Ansara. "Show up tomorrow after breakfast, Father Jim can show you where my store is, Hans." said Han's new boss, "I'll give you $5 a day, out of the extra expenses I was expecting to have for my store enlargement. I'll show you what to do. The job should be finished in about 4 days. I'll have the wife bring you a lunch, when she brings mine, we close at 5:30." "Oh. That would be great," said Hans. "Maybe by the 4 days I'll be able to find something more permanent." "Thank you very much," said Father Jim to Michael. "That's all right," said Michael, "I was wondering if I might have to close the store for 2 or 3 days, but now I won't."

After Mass Father Jim & Hans went to the rectory, where Marie had a nice breakfast fixed. As they sat down to eat, Father Jim said to Hans, Later on you will meet another priest, Father Salva. He's the part time priest for St. John the Baptist Church, about a 3 – hour drive to the east. He usually gets here at 5 o'clock," "He always gets here at 5 o'clock," said Marie. "I set my clock by him." "It was so nice to go to Mass again, and to receive the Lord's Body and Blood," said Hans, "do you have Mass every day? I've got a lot of time to make up for." "We don't have Mass on Saturday, tomorrow morning Father Salva will say the daily Mass. And I'll give you a rosary to say again, as you said you used to say it," said Father Jim.

So Hans met Father Salva later, and shared the spare room with him that night, as there were two beds in the room. In the morning Hans got up early, and went to the church at 7:30, to could say his new rosary before Mass. After Mass he went with Father Jim, as he drove him to Michael Ansara's store to begin his first day's work. Father Jim took some time before going fishing to stop and see the mayor, and tell him about his new guest. "You say he came from nowhere, how do you know he's Catholic?" said the Mayor. "Robert, he came to the rectory because he saw one of our signs about us wanting men singers, he used to sing in choir. He was dirty and disreputable looking from his travels, on foot. After getting cleaned up he confessed that he hadn't been to Mass for a while.

The next morning I heard his confession before daily Mass, he knew what to say. He looked very happy at Mass. I gave him a rosary, which he said the next morning before Father Salva did the Friday morning Mass. Mike Ansara hired him to help with his store for a few days." Said Father Jim. "Well, I just have to be careful of strangers," said the mayor. "I would like to know more about him," said Gerald Hooper, who had been listening in, along with his wife Martha, and their two youngest children, 4 year old Mary, and 3 year old Malon. "I want to make sure it's safe to have a stranger with us, especially with our five children," said Gerald. "Yes," said the mayor, "I know you want it safe for your children. Your oldest is Dora, she's what, 10?" asked the mayor. "No, she's eleven now," said Mr. Hooper. Kalex is nine, and Sally is six. Of course, they're all in school now, Mary will start school next Fall." "We do have to be careful because of the war," said Erika Floors, the mayor's secretary. "Remember the warning that President Roosevelt told of in his talks, that it is our civic duty to beware of anyone who looks like a German, or an Oriental. I heard on the news that on the west coast and in some other places, how many Americans of Japanese descent have been put into camps, away from their homes and businesses, until they can be cleared someday." "Yes, I've heard of that also," said the mayor. "And it doesn't seem right, in a way, if they are American citizens, but we are at war with Japan. I guess that our government isn't taking any chances." Just then 3 of the people who were there left the mayor's office. The mayor said, "They heard us talking, I hope they don't tell others that we might have a person who is dangerous in our midst." "Tell any person who thinks Hans is dangerous to come to me," said Father Jim. "I've found him to be a very decent, upright man, and someone who loves our Catholic Faith, even if he has been away from the Church for a while. There are some parishioners I could name who have missed Mass a few times, with no excuse for not attending."

So it ended there, any suspicions about Hans Kruger. But when Sunday came a few people talked to Father Jim before Mass, about the stranger who was staying at the rectory. Because Hans had worked at Michael Ansara's store on Friday and Saturday, many people had seen him, and pointed him out to others. As Mass was starting Father Jim noticed that where Hans sat, in the 3rd pew from the front, on the left, there were empty seats in the pew to both sides of Hans, and some empty seats in the pew behind him. Hans noticed this, after he finished saying his rosary. Father Jim noticed how the people were behaving, and tried to put an end to It in his homily. After a short version of the homily he had prepared, Father Jim went on by saying, "It is only God who judges. I welcome anyone who is willing to work to pay his own way, as Hans Kruger is doing now, as he shows every sign of being a good Catholic.

The main reason he came to us was to offer to sing for our choir. The choir will start to rehearse this Thursday night, with a somewhat larger choir, which has 5 men singers now, and 6 with Hans Kruger. And it is also the law of the land that everyone is innocent until proven guilty. I know you all remember the parable of the Good Samaritan; we, too, are called to be Good

Samaritans. If a man looked like he was of Japanese descent, I could understand you being hesitant to accept him, but he looks like the rest of us, except for his own personal differences, which we all have. Our God makes us all unique in this way. We are all members of Good Shepherd Church. Let us remember, Christ is remembered as the Good Shepherd, as He led the lowliest, neediest of God's children. Is it not up to us to do the same?" The people sat in silence as Father Jim went to the altar to finish the Mass. Father Jim's talk had changed the thinking of most of the people. It showed when, as the people left the church, several of them came up to Hans and shook his hand. But Father Jim noticed that there were still a few who walked away from Hans, as two families ushered their children out of church, away from Hans.

Back at the rectory Father Jim looked at Marie as she was fixing breakfast. Marie noticed the rather inquisitive look on Father Jim's face. "Oh, that was nice, what you said about Hans," said Marie. "Yes," said Father Jim, "many people, as they left, greeted me, and said they will welcome Hans into the parish. "And," said Father Jim to Hans, "I talked to Anthony Zerbee. He asked me how much longer you would be working at the store. He's a farmer. and needs someone to help him with his harvest, and for picking apples from his orchard, when they're ripe in about a week or so. Anthony has 4 children, Andrew is the oldest, he just finished school last June, and he has 3 younger girls, still in school. His son has been busy building a house on the farther part of the farm, to start up with farming himself, to have a house for himself and his bride; they will be married in late November. He says he will match the pay you're getting now, as well as food and board while you're at the farm, so you won't have to go back and forth to the rectory." "That would be nice," said Hans." "It will be for several weeks," said Father Jim, maybe until we get our first snow in October." "And I'll give you half of what I earn at the store, for all you've done for me." said Hans. "No, we don't do things for pay, at our church," said Father Jim.

The rest of the day was quiet, as Father Jim went to the church later on to say some private prayers, with Marie relaxing, and reading some chapters of the Bible. After Father Jim returned they both listened to the radio, and thanked God for turning many people away from distrust and hatred in church. But Father Jim knew he still had to pay some visits to some parishioners who were still not persuaded that the stranger from nowhere was not an evil man, not a danger.

Chapter 4

Monday and Tuesday were the last two days for Hans with his job at Michael Ansara's store. Wednesday morning Father Jim brought Hans to the farm he would be working at, as Hans had some new farm clothes he had bought with some of the $20 he had earned at the store.

"I won't be able to make it to daily Mass anymore," said Hans to Fr. Jim. "But you can come with the family for Sunday Mass," said Father Jim. "They're a good family, they never miss Sunday Mass, except for some days in the winter, when we have a big snow that stops even some people from making it, some even closer than the Zerbee family. I give them all absolution for this, but most of them still come to confession as soon as they can, so they can confess missing Mass, so that they will feel right for receiving communion. As I absolve them of their sins, and give them a light penance, I think to myself, "this person is not far from God."

When Father Jim got back to the rectory he said to Marie, "It looks like Hans is all set in his new job, but I still need to get to work and make sure our parishioners will accept our good friend Hans into the parish, and also in the community. People who don't accept Hans as a fellow Christian could mean trouble for Hans, and also endanger their own soul." "You are right," said Marie. "Does this mean we will have to talk to people outside of church?" "Yes, there isn't much time to talk to them in church,' said Father Jim. "I'll make a list of the ones who apparently weren't convinced by the little talk I gave, after the homily. And we can also go to some of the businesses, or places where people congregate." "How about the library?" said Marie. "Yes, a lot of people go there." Said Father Jim. "The librarian, Miriam Widdis, isn't a Catholic, but she's still a good woman, and she should be able to change some stubborn people's minds. Everyone respects your librarian, as they are often more educated than an average person," said Father Jim. "I have two books that are due back in a few days, I'll bring them back tomorrow, and make sure she knows the truth about Hans," said Marie. "That's fine," said Father Jim. But I still need to make a list of the people who were not convinced by my talk. I can think of four of our families, offhand, can you write down any you know of?" asked Father Jim. "Yes, I know of two families whose parents were pushing their children out of church, away from Hans," said Marie. "Yes, I saw them, too," said Father Jim. "I'll put them first on my list of people to visit." "It will be a little different than your usual visit," said Marie. "Yes, it will be a sort of a challenge, but a priest needs to do whatever it takes to help the sheep of his flock, whether it's a pleasant, social event where I sometimes stay for supper, or it's for something like this, where the people aren't going to like what I have to say about their way of thinking," said Father Jim.

So Father Jim started writing up a list of people to see. "I'll have to go after 6:30, since most people are working during the day. And, as most of them don't have a telephone, I'll have to make more than one trip for many of them. Their kids, or a neighbor, will at least be able to tell me when they'll be home," said Father Jim.

After an hour Father Jim had a list made of people who probably weren't swayed by his talk of being a Good Samaritan, and not judging others. "Eli Bancroft, the tax man is the first one I'll go to," said Father Jim. He was one who made sure his children didn't have a chance to meet Hans. Robert Taylor is next, he did the same thing with his kids." "Earl Hanmer is a farmer who lives on the edge of town," said Marie, "he also walked out if church pretty fast, and so did Patricia Blare, who was at Mass without her husband; he only comes once in a while. I'm sure she told him what she thought of our stranger."

So, next morning, after breakfast, Marie left the rectory to take her books back to the library, where she would inform their librarian, Miriam Widdis, of the problem with a few people in their church who had the wrong idea of a good man who had come to stay with them, & was now working on the Zerbee farm. Father Jim took his list and went to a few men, and a few women, who would be at work in a tailor shop or a bakery. He first went to see Matt Masterson, a hunter who did odd jobs on the side. Matt was getting ready to go hunting, but he agreed to listen to his pastor. "I know you were at Mass on Sunday," said Father, "I couldn't help but notice that you walked away without welcoming our new parishioner." "I don't cotton to strangers, especially one who comes from nowhere," said Matt. "But don't you realize we were all strangers at one time? Everyone has to start somewhere," said Father Jim. "I know the man. He's a good Catholic who has been away from the Church for a while, but not of his own choosing. He was overjoyed to be able to go to Mass again, and to receive holy communion, after I heard his confession." You know Mike Ansara, Hans did good work for him in his store and is now working at the Zerbee farm. But most of all, he's a good Catholic who will be singing in our choir. Please, do me, and yourself, a favor by meeting with him after Mass on Sunday, to let him know you will be his friend. Our Lord teaches us to love our fellow man." Father Jim could see that he had succeeded in in changing the hunter's opinion of Hans. "You're right," said Matt. "I will do as our Lord teaches and talk to him after Mass, and be a friend." "That's fine," said Father Jim. "There are a few others who think as you did. If you hear anyone saying anything bad about Hans, tell them what I told you, you'll be doing God's work."

Father left Matt Masterson, as the hunter went out on a quest for some game for himself, and for a grocery store that buys meat from him to sell. At his next two stops only one parent was there, and in one case neither parent, as the father was working, and the mother was out running some errands, with the grandmother there to look after the children. But he talked to a single parishioner who seemed reluctant to hear Father Jim at first, but said, as Father left, that he would try to think about what Father had said, and would at least introduce himself to Hans after Mass.

Coming home for lunch father Jim told Marie how he did in his talks with parishioners. "I did good with Miriam," said Marie. "She said she does keep an open mind for everything, that it comes with a lot of reading. She said she would help us with any doubters about our new man." "That is great!" said Father Jim. I have confessions from 1 to 3, then I'll come back and figure out who to go to tonight.

At 5 o'clock Father Jim had finished with his list of people to go to after supper. Father Salva came, and Marie pulled Father Jim to the side and said to him, "Father Salva doesn't know anything about our problem with some people about Hans, I think we should tell him, he will be saying Mass tomorrow morning, and hearing confessions after breakfast. We need to let him know what's going on." Then Father Salva joined Father Jim and Marie at the table and said: "I think I know about the problem you might be having, about Hans." "You know?" asked Father Jim. "Yes," said Father Salva, "last Sunday one of my parishioners was visiting some family members here, and went to Mass with them at Good Shepherd. She told me that she wasn't sure about a stranger coming to church, when he hadn't been to Mass for a long time. I told her that I knew Hans personally, and that he was a good Catholic, and friend, and that we shouldn't think of him in a negative way. She said she would ignore what she heard when she heard someone refer to him as a bad man." "Good, said Father Jim, "I know that word of something like this gets around. Marie went to our librarian and told her about Hans, so that she will straighten out anyone who thinks bad things about Hans. And I've been going around to a few places this morning, to some of our parishioners, I'm going out tonight to tell some others of Hans, some who work during the day. "Maybe you should tell the mayor about him," said Father Salva. "Oh, he is a parishioner, I already told him about Hans, he'll tell anyone who comes to see him," said Father Jim. "Well, how about those who grow flowers, and raise vegetables?" said Marie. "They're good at knowing the truth in gossip." "What makes you say that?" said Father Jim. "Why Father, you surprise me," said Marie. "Don't you know that gardeners know all the best dirt?" Father Salva chuckled, & Father Jim shook his head and said," I think it's time for you to go to confession, Marie." Marie just smiled, she knew Father didn't really mean she should go to confession. As Father Salva still smiled, he said: "Oh, that's a good one, Marie. I'll have to remember that, when I go back to St. John's."

They had supper, Marie had fixed chili for tonight, something they rarely had. After supper Father Jim got his list of people to go to, and went to one of the families who ushered their kids out of church, and others who lived in the same neighborhood. The other parents who ushered their kids out of church lived on the other part of town, he would see them on Friday night. Friday was one of Father Jim's two days off, but he knew that it was important to nip this thing in the bud, before others were told that a dangerous stranger was loose in the community.

About 8:30 Father Jim came back, he had talked to the parents who had shoved their kids away from Hans. They seemed to be convinced that wasn't dangerous, but they seemed like they weren't 100% convinced. At least they promised not to say anything bad about Hans. At the next house Father's talk about Hans was well – received. They said they were thinking of not coming to Mass because of Hans, but now they would. At the next house only the husband was home, his wife was visiting with a nearby neighbor. So Father told him about Hans, the man said he would pass it on to his wife. The man said he would, he was convinced about Hans. At the last house the man and wife both listened to Father's talk, but they didn't say anything until one of their kids came to Father and said that they would like to meet the new singer in the choir. Father Jim assured him that Hans would be glad to meet him, with his parents. At this the parents looked at each other, then said that they would take their children to meet the new singer in their choir.

"Things are looking up," said Father Jim to Marie. "I'll still have to go to more places tomorrow, starting with the other parents who ushered their kids out of church." "But, it's your day off," said Marie. "Getting our parishioners into a proper way of thinking is more important than another fishing trip," said Father Jim. "I told my people that they should be a good shepherd, I would be neglect in my duty if I didn't do the same."

So, after breakfast Father Jim set out to see the other people on his list, when he would normally be fishing with the mayor and several children from the mayor's, and other families. Father Jim went first to the one other family whose kids were ushered out of the church, but didn't make a good impression, since the father was out hunting. Father Jim had to talk to the mother, but she seemed convinced that there was nothing to fear about the new man named Hans. "But," said the woman, "I'll have to talk about what you said with my husband, and he doesn't always listen to what I say."

As Father Jim went on to other places on this side of town, the next Place was vacant, the whole family had gone somewhere. So Father left a note on the door, saying that he wished to talk to them, after Mass on Sunday. He found three others on his list home, and all were pleased to have him visit, and listened to Father tell them about their new member in the parish. Marie had fixed Father Jim a sandwich and some other items to have for lunch, since he would be out until mid – afternoon. But when Fr. Jim stopped at one house just before noon, the family insisted that he stay and have lunch with them. When Father Jim told them why he was there, they assured him that they would welcome Hans, that they hadn't met him before, but they would make an effort to see him this Sunday.

It was after 3 when Father got back to the rectory. He gave the lunch Marie had fixed him back to her, and she put it back in the icebox. She also told him that he could take two names off his list. After Father Salva was done with the stations of the Cross, he came to the rectory and greeted 4 different parishioners, some of whom Father Jim wanted to see about Hans. Fr. Salva told them about Hans, and they left, satisfied with what they heard. Their names were recorded on the parish records, for parishioner visits, and two of them were on Father Jim's list. "Well, that just leaves 3 who we need to see." said Father Jim, "and I'm sure they will be at Mass on Sunday. In my homily I'll briefly mention how I've visited," "Well," said Marie, this makes one time when Father Salva did something besides eat us out of food." "With at least 5 families that I talked to are coming to Mass," said Father Jim, "I'm sure that at least a few others will see that Hans is not a leper, and some who are still a little bit suspicious will come around.

Things were good for Sunday Mass, as Father Jim asked the parishioners at the end of Mass if they enjoyed their new, larger choir, with their newest man singer, Hans Kruger. as the songs sung in 4-part harmony sounded better now for their celebration of the Eucharist. Many people, mostly the ones Father Jim had talked to, went to meet Hans, after he had stepped away from the other choir members.

Back at the rectory Hans told Father Jim and Marie how happy he was about his life here, after traveling for many miles through the countryside, with very little to eat, and no contact with his God at Mass, just the personal private prayers he said, as he thanked God for just being alive.

After Hans sat down to eat, Father Jim asked him how his job was going. "Oh, it's fine," said Hans, "we've been getting in hay, and some straw, and corn. And Anthony says that in a week or so the apples will be ready for picking. He pays me at the end of the day. I've got enough money to buy another pair of pants; the ones I have are getting pretty worn. I'll get another shirt,

also. I put one day's wages, $5, in the collection to help out."
"That's generous," said Fr. Jim. Most of our people can't afford more than a dollar in these times, many put not much more than a quarter, or a dime." "Well, as long as I'm working I'll put in a day's pay each Sunday. I also talked to some of the people after Mass, who welcomed me to the parish. Two of the men, and a 16 year old said they would like to join our choir," said Hans. "Oh," said Hans, "and Mr. Zerbee says he's very satisfied with my work. And, I went one day to see how his son Andrew was doing with the house he's building, I went there with his future wife, Cora Ryan. She was also interested in how the house was doing. Then Andrew asked me if I could help him with his house after the apples were picked, so the house would be ready to live in by the time he was married. He said he would arrange for me to get something from his father for helping me out, so the house would be finished on time. He said they were getting married just before Thanksgiving. And Cora invited me to their wedding. It's been about four years since I went to a wedding." "That's wonderful!" said Father Jim. "I still think of when you first came here, how down and out you were. But you've put your trust in the Lord, and He hasn't let you down. And when word gets around about what a reliable, trusty worker you are, you might be able to afford a small house for yourself, and maybe even meet a good woman to share your life with." "Well, I'm just taking things day by day for now," said Hans. "But when I saw Andrew and Cora together, I think it would be the best way for me, also, with a good woman." "Oh, that would be nice," said Marie, "I know of several young, unattached women in the parish."

After supper Father Jim took Hans back to the Zerbee farm, for another 6 days of work, which would make him $30 richer, since he seldom had a chance to spend any of it, since he was out in the country all week. And Father Jim used Hans as an example when he talked to a one of his parishioners who was having financial problems. And these people, who were a bit leery of a man simply because he was a stranger, were all better

Catholics for listening to their pastor. And with three more men joining the choir, there was finally a good man/ woman balance for the 4 part harmony songs that the 24 member choir sang for Mass. "Who knew what one dirty, worn out stranger's coming to our parish would make." said Father Jim to Marie one morning. "God does work in mysterious ways."

Chapter 5

The days seemed to be going faster as the activities of the harvest, and the acceptance of Hans by everybody was welcomed. Hans was still working on the Zerbee farm, and glad to be like a member of the family, as the Zerbee family was happy to take him to Good shepherd for Mass on Sunday, and to his Thursday night choir rehearsal with the other choir members. And Hans was saving his money; he looked forward to buying or renting a house of his own in the town, so that he could more easily get to his work, possibly with a horse.

It was Sunday, Hans was with Father Jim and Marie for breakfast. Hans sat there as he ate, not saying anything, with an apprehensive look on his face. "Is everything going good on the farm," asked Father Jim. "Oh yes," said Hans, we're almost done with picking apples. There will still be some work to do with getting the hay into the barn, but after that I might go to work for Andrew, to help him get his house built, in time for their wedding. Hans' father told him, he could pay me $3 a day for helping his son, as part of his wedding gift to him. So, everything there is fine, but I've been doing a lot of thinking lately, Father, and I need to come to you and clear up something with a special confession, just you and me." "You need to go to confession?" asked Father Jim. "Well, it's not a regular confession, not like the one I went to with you the first time, before I went to the first Mass I had been to in a long time," said Hans. "No, I need to see you alone, I have some things I need to tell you that might not actually be sins, but things I need to tell you about," said

Hans. "You go fishing Saturday in the morning, don't you?" "Yes," said Father Jim, "does this have something to do with fishing?" "No," said Hans, "but if I could be here Saturday morning and go fishing with you, it wouldn't upset your schedule, as we could be by ourselves for my confession. I'll tell Anthony I need Saturday off, to take care of some personal business. I can have him drop me off Friday night, after supper, I can still sleep in the same room I was staying in before, can't I?" "Yes," said Father Jim. Then we can go fishing after breakfast as you always do. Be sure to bring the things you usually have for confession, I want this to still count as a private talk, then you won't be able to say anything I tell you to anyone else." "I can't but help wonder why you want to do it this way," said Father Jm. "When we have our "confession talk' you will understand why I'm doing it this way," said Hans. "All right, I'll be looking for you Friday night, we can take it from there," said Father Jim. Are you sure Anthony can get along without you for Saturday?" "Yes, I already told him I might need to take a day off, he said it would be all right, but without pay," said Hans.

So, when Father Salva came on Thursday, Father Jim told him that he had something to do Saturday morning, to make sure that Father Salva would take care of the confessions, and the stations of the Cross, and anything else that came up. "Sure, I'll be here for you," said Father Salva, "but I thought you usually go fishing on Saturday." "I will be going fishing, but I will be with Hans, to talk over a few things with me," said Father Jim. "Can you tell me what it's all about?" asked Father Salva. "No, it's a personal matter. Just take care of things, I should be back in time for lunch," said Father Jim.

On Friday evening Anthony Zerbee drove up in his old 1936 Chevy pickup, and dropped off Hans Kruger. Hans said hello to Father Jim, and Marie, and went into the living room to talk with Father Jim for a while, as he stressed the importance of their special confession, assuring him that he would understand why he was doing the confession this way.

The next morning, Marie fixed a tasty breakfast, with the usual seconds for Father Salva. "I can fix you a couple of sandwiches, and some iced tea if you think you'll be there past noon," said Marie. "Well," said Fr. Jim to Hans, "do you think we'll be finished in time to get back by noon? The forecast is for rain later on, so it would be best if we could make our fishing trip a short one." "Yes, I'm sure we'll be done by 11 AM, unless we get too busy pulling in a lot of fish," said Hans. "Well, if that's the case, we can stop fishing until we're done with our talk," said Father Jim.

When Father Jim and Hans came to their usual fishing spot they saw that Robert Horton, the mayor, was already there with his kids, and Chuck Connor, a farmer, and hunter, along with Newly O'Brien, a gunsmith, and a few children Father Jim didn't recognize. There wasn't much room for Father Jim and Hans there anyway, they knew they would need to go to some other places anyway. The mayor & Chuck said hello to Hans, this was the first time in a while they had seen him outside of church "We're not going to get any fish with all of you here," said Father Jim, to the mayor. "Hans and I will go upstream a ways and find us a place there. We just might get some fish before they get to you" "Good luck," said the mayor.

So Father Jim and Hans did go upstream, and found a good spot for fishing, about 30 feet away from the others. "We can have our talk here," said Father Jim, "with no one else hearing us." "But we must first bait our hook and cast our line into the water," said Hans. "Yes, hand me a worm," said Father Jim, "we'll get started with our fishing." After they had both cast their lines into the stream they sat down and Father Jim asked Hans what he wanted to tell him. "No, Father, not until you put on your, is it a stole?" said Hans. "I still want this to be a private confession, even though it will be a lot more than confessing my sins." Father Jim complied, so that it was, for now. as if he were back in church, in the confessional.

After the usual beginning for a confession, Hans said his special sin. "I have had thoughts of killing people since I was taken into the army. I was taught to kill the British, and Americans," said Hans. "What," said Father Jim, "you were taught to kill your own people?" "No," said Hans, "I was in the German army, as soon as I finished high school. I grew up in the Bavarian part of Germany, which is why I'm Catholic, many of the people in Bavaria are Catholics.

After three weeks of basic training I was sent to fight the British in north Africa, and the Americans who were just joining the British in the fight for control of Africa, and hopefully, the Suez Canal, which was still in control of the British. They told us that if Hitler could gain control of the Suez Canal he could block off all Allied shipping through the canal." "Oh, yes, I know what you mean," said Father Jim, "I know of the Suez Canal." "Our German armies controlled most of north Africa, and our own general, called Rommel, was pushing hard to win over the British forces, but couldn't get control of Egypt," said Hans. They said he was like a fox, in the way he won many battles in the desert. But, Father, I was a good Catholic, and was saddened with the way Hitler was closing some of our churches, and taking some priests away to unknown place, and were never heard from again. We had a building, a few miles of the Mediterranean coast, where an SS group was training specially picked men to learn English, and of the main cities in the United States and Britain, so they could be sent there by our submarines, to get any information that they could pass on to certain agents, which would get, in turn, passed on to Germany to help Germany in the war effort.

There were 18 of us, 3 already knew some English, and learned to speak it faster than the rest, except for me. I had taken up a special class in English in high school, and knew the language well, with only a slight German accent. But as I learned more, I could speak without an accent, so they had plans for me, since I was the best in the class for speaking English. They said that in another week or so they were going to arrange for us to be put on a sub, which would sneak through the Gibraltar Strait, while the Luftwaffe made an attack on British forces there to distract them. Then I would be taken to the east coast of the United

States to wait for some of our underground people to give me fake IDs, and get me to Washington, D. C., Where I would try to get into the Pentagon, passing as a loyal American." "Yes," said Father Jim, "we know that Germany, and Japan, as well, have spies in the United States, and in Britain. We also have spies of our own in Europe, and Japan, as well. That's the way it is in a big war like the one we're in.

Some of our brave volunteers for this pass on important facts to us, and sadly, some of them are discovered, and we never see them again, unless, they are eventually freed from a prisoner of war camp. But they are heroes, as much as the ones fighting in the battlefield, or at sea. It was in our papers a while ago how our navy turned back the strong Japanese navy, as Japan tried to take over a small atoll in the Pacific, called Midway Island. As some losses were reported for some of our ships, planes, and pilots, it was reported that Japan lost even more ships, planes, and pilots, and because of this, we can be sure that Japan will never again try to attack us across the big Pacific with their forces." "I didn't know about that," said Hans. "I seldom saw a newspaper. Oh, as I said, I had bad feelings about what Germany was doing, especially with the SS closing our churches, and taking away Jews, our priests, and others who weren't part of the "Master Race", to unknown places. I was beginning to wonder if I could do my job as a spy for a nation that treated its people with so much disrespect. But I never got the chance, thank God, as the British and American armies launched a surprise attack on us, which was so big that it pushed the main part of our army back, while they encircled our four divisions, forcing us to surrender. We were all taken back to the east and put on ships or planes to a few places in Britain, but I think most of us were sent to the United States, to several prisoner of war camps there. I knew that there were several camps, because I heard several guards talking about them. Of course, they didn't know I could understand them, as I didn't say anything. It was late April, maybe the beginning of May, when I and several hundred of my countrymen were brought to Camp Gruber. It's somewhere in Okal, or Okelhoma, some state like that." "Do you mean Oklahoma?" said Father Jim. "Yes! that's it, Oklahoma," said Hans. "Many of us talked in defiance to the guards. A few who could speak broken English said to them, "Just wait until Hitler gets here, we'll fix you!" "Oh my gosh," said Father Jim, "do you mean that some men actually thought that Hitler would come over to America to free them?" "Yes, you see, many of them had seen Hitler go across Europe at will, they looked at their Fuhrer as an invincible leader," said Hans, so I thought to myself, as I spent more than two weeks in Camp Gruber, how Hitler was thousands of miles away, and was having his hands full with just holding on to Africa, the fallacy of Germany trying to cross the Atlantic, without being attacked by U. S. forces. They would, I reasoned, never get to the U. S. shore, much less take over the very large United States. But some men still thought Hitler was unbeatable. I was careful not to say any words in English, for fear the prisoners would think I was an undercover guard. But I did hear of an escape attempt being planned, by four other inmates. I joined them to get out before someone discovered that I could speak English. A guard had been bribed, and late at night we were able to make it over the wall. Three of them ran right away, as the siren sounded, and the outside lights flooded the area. The other man went to the right, I went to the left, and hid in some bushes, until the coast was clear enough for me to make it to a bridge, where I hid for the night. I heard the tower guard announcing that they had caught 4 of the escapees, and that they thought that that was all of them. So I ate a sandwich I had brought from lunch, and went away at night to find a store with clothes, so I could get in and get rid of my prison garb, and put on regular clothes, and a pair of shoes. From there on I became a lonely traveler, as I went north, to get farther away from the prison. I'm sure that when the prison did a head count they realized I was missing, but I was way too far from them to find me by then." "But how did you survive out there by yourself?" asked Fr. Jim. "I just remembered some of the survival training they gave us in the basic training. The new clothes I got from the store looked good for a few weeks, I even made some money from a store owner by helping him one day because his regular helper was away. My clothes did get dirty when I helped a farmer in his field. But I just kept going north. No one suspected me of being an escaped prisoner of war because my English was so good. So, you see, I can't come forth and become a United States citizen, as I wish I could, because the government would find out who I am. Can you figure out any way I could become a United States citizen, without getting myself put back in prison, Father?" asked Hans. "I can't think of anything right now. Dealing with a prisoner of war isn't something we deal with in the seminary," said Father Jim. "But I'll try to find out something, without saying why I'm asking." "You can't tell anyone who I am," said Hans, "I was in a confession with you, which means it's only between you and me."

"And God," said Fr. Jim "I will do some praying to ask for guidance for the situation." "Yes," said Hans, "because even though you're a priest, you could be in serious trouble for this, because we're at war." "I know," said Father Jim, "I could be in deep trouble with the government, and probably with the Church, also."

Father Jim sat back to think about the situation, this was something he didn't think he would ever have to deal with. Then, he realized his fishing rod was being pulled down to the water's edge. He grabbed the pole, and pulled in a nice bass. Then he saw that Hans was also pulling in a fish, a big pike. "We didn't even know we had a fish on our line,' said Hans. "No, and it's after 11 o'clock," said Father Jim. "We had better put our poles away and start back to the rectory. I never came back with just one fish before." "Well, I only have one also," said Hans. "We were there, talking, for about two hours," said Father Jim. "That's the longest confession I've ever had." "Remember, what I told you is just between you and me, and God," said Hans. "Yes, I'll keep my priestly vow of silence for it," said Father Jim.

On the way back to the rectory Hans told Father Jim about some of the places he had been to, and the jobs he had done for a meal, and for a place to sleep, usually in a barn, or for enough money to buy himself a meal. Father Jim said that he would say a rosary for him, and to help him with a solution to Hans' problem. As they went into the kitchen Marie had lunch fixed. Father Salva was already seated, with a plate full of spaghetti in front of him. "Is that all you have?" said Marie, as she saw the 2 fish Father Jim and Hans had. "Yes," said Father Jim, "we had a very relaxing time, the fish just weren't biting much, maybe because of the new spot we went to. It was too crowded where we usually go. The mayor and two other men were there, and several children took up most of the places for fishing." "Well, put the fish in the crisper in the icebox for now," said Marie, "and wash up. Father Salva said that since you weren't here he would say the blessing, and start eating his first helping of spaghetti."

So they had a nice spaghetti supper, with homemade meatballs and a loaf of fresh – baked Italian bread. Father Salva left soon after supper to get back to his parish, to get ready for Sunday Mass at St. John's. Father Jim and Hans then went into the living room to talk some more about Hans' "confession", and how they would pray for the Lord's guidance in finding an answer to a problem not usually found in the world, especially in a time of war. They would put it in God's hands.

Chapter 6

So, things continued on as before at Good Shepherd with Father Jim, as Hans continued working on the Zerbee farm, as he worked for less pay as he did work for Andrew Zerbee, to finish the foundation for the new house Andrew was building for he and his new wife, after they were married. They then started working on the roof, and the walls of some of the rooms. Hans continued to think of what he had told Father Jim, and prayed for a solution. He went to church early enough on Sunday to say an extra rosary, which he offered up for a solution to his problem. Before going to sing in choir again. The other choir members saw him doing a lot of praying, but just figured it was for something he was doing in thanks, or for something else he had to pray for.

"So, how's everything going with Andrew Zerbee's house?" said Father Jim to Hans, shortly after he got to the rectory on Saturday night. "Oh, enough of it is done so that Andrew doesn't need my help anymore," said Hans, "and, last week after Mass Dan Blocker of the ranch by the edge of town said that he could use my help with his horses and cattle, if I could do the job of a rancher. He said he would give me $4 a day, for a 6-day week, and I could come to Mass with him on Sunday." "Yes, I know him," said Father Jim," it might be a good experience for you." "I'm going to ask Dan when he wants me to start," said Hans, "I've done farming, I should be able to do a ranch job."

After Sunday Mass, Hans came to Father Jim and told him that Dan Blocker said that he could use me right away, or as soon as I could get to his ranch. "That's good," said Father Jim, "it looks like things are going good for you and your new life here. "Yes," said Hans, "and one of the good things with this is with our choir. I found a new man who is joining the choir, Flint McCull, a good base, and two more women, Loretta Switt, and Maggie Ebsen. That will give us 10 men, 14 women. Our balance will be good for our 4-part harmony." "That's great," said Father Jim. "Yes, and we've been getting some compliments from people for some of the new songs, as well as some of the old favorites that our choir leader, Chester Good, has picked out for us," "As we get into October you'll be planning some songs for Advent, and Christmas," said Father Jim. I can remember when I first came here, there were eleven choir members, 8 women, and only 3 men. Now, we sound almost like a choir you hear in a cathedral." As Father Jim looked at Hans, he said again, "Almost as good."

That night Han's new employer, Dan Blocker, picked up Hans and took him out to his ranch. But before he left Hans again asked Father Jim to keep on praying for a solution to his problem. Hans rode in Dan's truck to a place where he would continue to work, and make himself known to the community as a responsible, dependable man. He found out that his employer didn't go anyplace but on his ranch, except for an occasional trip to town for business. But a friend who lived down the road was in the choir, and would stop by and pick up Hans to go to rehearsal on Thursday night. Hans would go with the Blocker family on Sunday to Mass. Hans liked music, ever since he had sung in chorus in high school. And he liked the chorus they had in his church in Bavaria, until the Germans closed his church, and then took away both of their priests. At times Hans pretended that he was singing in his former church, as he did his best to sing the songs that the congregation enjoyed so much, especially for songs that hadn't been sung in their church for a while, that fit in with their Mass for the day. Hans was a good base, with three others, and six tenors, to make a good harmony with the six altos and eight sopranos. When the choir sang in unison the sopranos seemed to carry the song, but people could also hear the six altos, and the ten men.

Father Jim said that he was always glad to see Hans after Mass, he always told him how nice the choir sounded, especially when they sang an old favorite, Amazing Grace, for the recessional. Hans then said," I thought Immaculate Mary was a good song for communion, also." Father nodded, he said he got compliments each week from parishioners, about the good music from the Good Shepherd Choir. When Father Jim called the Bishop for his weekly report, he said that he wished he could make it to Good Shepherd sometime to hear their choir. The Bishop replied that he was used to hearing more than 30 voices in the choir the cathedral had, but that he would try to come for a visit, maybe sometime during the Advent season. "That would be fine," said Father Jim, "it's been about three years since you graced us with a visit." "I wasn't aware it had been that long," said the Bishop, "I always get a good report from Bishop O'Hanlon, I guess that it's about time to see things for myself, especially since you have a larger choir now."

"Well, I had a nice talk with the Bishop," said Father Jim to Marie, "he said he would check his schedule, and come for a visit, maybe during Advent." "That will be nice," said Marie, "many of our younger children have never seen him, except for the picture you have of him, beside the picture of Pope Pius XII, in the living room, and many haven't been there to see that. Almost half of our parishioners have a picture of the Pope in their home, but only a handful have one of the Bishop. Do you think he'll like our choir?" "I'm sure he will, even though he has a larger choir at the cathedral," said Father Jim. "By the way," said Marie, "have you noticed how Hans acts sometimes? He's happy to be able to go to Mass again, and to sing in choir, but he seems to be worried about something. I've noticed how he goes to Mass early, and says the rosary not once, but twice, before going and joining the others in the choir." "Well, he has a lot to think about, because of the way he came to us, the different jobs he's been working at, and what will be ahead of him for his life. He talked with Andrew Zerbee a lot while he was working with him, he told me how impressed he was that Andrew was going to marry a good woman," said Father Jim, I think he might just be thinking of meeting a girl on one of his jobs, or even in church. He's a young man who I'm sure would like to have a good woman, if he finds one." "I guess there's always a chance to meet a woman in Good Shepherd," said Marie, maybe that's why he prays so much. He will make some woman a good husband someday."

A few days later the Bishop called, and talked to Father Jim for about five minutes. Marie looked expectantly at Father Jim after he hung up the phone. "Well, it's all set," said Father Jim, "the Bishop says he'll leave Bishop O'Hanlon in charge, and come to see us on the 3rd Sunday of Advent." "My, the Bishop does plan for things ahead of time," said Marie. "Marie, he says he already has plans for next year's Lent, & Easter Sunday," said Father Jim." "And to think, we don't usually plan for things past the rest of the month," said Marie. "Well, a bishop always has more things going on than a parish priest. Actually, I'm surprised he could squeeze us in during Advent," said Father Jim, as he went to the calendar to mark the 3rd Sunday of Advent as the date they would have the Bishop with them. As October came to an end, a nice Mass for All Saint's Day was said, with some parishioners closing their businesses for the morning, almost like a national holiday. Andrew Zerbee started getting ready for their wedding, on the last Saturday before Thanksgiving. Andrew was still working on his house, but he would have everything but a few final details done before the wedding. When Father Jim told the choir about the Bishop visiting them on the 3rd Sunday of Advent, the choir leader got together with the choir members to decide on some special songs to sing for the Bishop, ones that they thought he might not have heard for a while, but still having one or two of the good old hymns that everyone loved to hear. While trying to think of some good songs to sing, Chester

Good went to Hans to ask him if he had any good songs he had heard, I should be in the church that he came from. "Well, I did not sing in choir for the last two years I was there," said Hans, while not mentioning that the Germans had closed his church, "but I do remember something different than we have here. The problem would be getting a music for it," as he carefully didn't say anything about his church being in Germany. "Shall we go back to looking through this pile of hymnals that we haven't used yet?" said Chester. "Oh yes, I'm sure we will find something in them," said Hans, "we should be able to find something there to have for a good recessional for the Bishop" "And we should have two or three songs to sing before Mass," said Chester, "maybe some old Christmas favorites like Away in a Manger."

After their rehearsal, and a brief search through the old hymnals to find something good to sing for the Bishop, Hans asked the friend who gave him a ride that night if he could stop at the rectory for a few minutes. "Sure," said Barbara Eden, a seamstress who lived close to the Blocker, "I'll just wait out front, no hurry."

Hans knocked with the front door's large metal knocker, and Marie came to the door. "Why, come in,' said Marie, "oh, Father, we have a visitor." Father Jim came in the room and greeted Hans. "Well Hans, is the rehearsal over?" asked Father Jim. "Yes, I need to talk to you, alone," said Hans." Marie went back to the kitchen, as Hans and Father Jim sat down on the couch, as Father Jim paid close attention to Hans, since he had a serious look on his face. "I almost made a big mistake, it would have been a serious one," said Hans." "What are you talking about?" asked Father Jim." "Chester Good came to me, some others have been trying to find good songs for when the Bishop comes, Chester knew that I had been in another church," said Hans, "I told him about a Bavarian folk song we used to sing." "Oh, no," said Father Jim, "you shouldn't say anything in reference to your previous life in Germany." "I know," said Hans, "it just sort of slipped out. But I don't think Chester even knows that Bavaria is a part of Germany. He didn't say anything, just went on to look for songs in the other hymnals." "I guess no harm was done," said Father Jim, but be careful not to say anything about where you were before you came here. If anyone asks you again about your former church, just tell them you don't want to talk about the past. I'll make things up by telling about someone I know of when I was in the Seminary, about someone who used to be in Germany years ago. I'm used to talking to people about things like this, but you might get nervous and try and make an excuse, and make it worse." "All right Father," said Hans, "I just had to tell you. I have to go, Barbara's waiting to take me back to the ranch."

So Hans continued his work on the ranch, and came with the Blockers for Sunday Mass. He continued saying two rosaries before Mass, and asked God to guide him. He enjoyed singing in choir, and felt close to God again, as he once again did his part for the sacrifice of the Mass.

Chapter 7

As the weeks passed there was no more trouble about Hans and his problem. It was getting close to Thanksgiving, and the wedding with Andrew Zerbee and Cora Ryan. Father Jim had already had a couple of meetings with the couple, as was usual before a man and woman get married in the Church. Andrew and Cora had graduated from high school last June, but had known each other since 8th grade. Andrew was raised a member of Good Shepherd, but Cora just became Catholic during her senior year. Her parents were both Methodists, but were not churchgoers. So they reluctantly let their daughter take RCIA classes so she could be a member of Good Shepherd. She received her first communion, and was confirmed in a special class run by Father Jim, with the permission of the Bishop, just before she graduated. Her parents knew that she and Andrew would be getting married, so they gave their blessing to the marriage, though they would remain Protestant, along with Cora's younger brother and sister. Father Jim told Marie that they would make a good couple, and would certainly have a lasting marriage, especially since Cora had converted for Andrew's sake, and seemed truly drawn to the Catholic Church.

Both families were busy getting ready for the wedding, as invitations were sent out, and Andrew and Cora personally drove Andrew's father's truck up to the Blocker ranch to personally bring an invitation to Hans. Hans had already bought a nice wedding gift for them. He had gotten to know Cora when he was working to help Andrew with his house, they were good friends. Hans thought about how happy they would be, sharing their life together, and that it would be nice if he could also find a nice woman who would love him, as much as he knew Cora loved Andrew.

The time came on the Thursday before thanksgiving, for the Good Shepherd choir to meet for their last rehearsal before Sunday, and also for some of the special songs they would sing on Saturday morning for Andrew's and Cora's wedding, Andrew had asked Hans if he would join him, on the groom's side of the church, behind his family members. "The choir can get along without you for one day, can't they?" said Andrew. "Oh yes, we have enough men to fill in for one less," said Hans. "When we only had 3 men in the choir, one less base or tenor would have made a difference." "Well, since you came to work for my father, and then with me, you've been almost like family," said Andrew, "and it's because of your help that the house is just about done. My father and my mother fixed up a large bed that they hadn't used for a while and gave it to me and Cora for our bedroom. He also found a medium sized dresser that we can use to put some of our clothes in, for now. Two boxes that had held feed would do for now for the rest of our clothes."

The rehearsal went well, the rest of the choir was singing songs for the wedding, without Hans, since he would be in the front of the church with the family. The next day was a busy one, as both families of the wedding couple were getting a few things done, including receiving a few friends and relatives from out of town who were coming to witness the wedding. A barn owned by a farmer, Gary Couper, that was sometimes used for a barn dance, would be used for the reception, after the wedding. Marion Ross, who worked as a cook, was a friend of the bride to be, was baking the large wedding cake, a 3 level one with the names of the bride and groom on it. Cora's mother Linda offered to pay for it, but Marion insisted on doing it as her gift. One last rehearsal with Fr. Jim was done in the morning, with the best man, the maid of honor, and the ring bearer, along with the parents, and others in the wedding party.

At the Couper barn tables and chairs were set up, with preparations made for food to be cooked after the wedding Mass, with one table set aside for the guests to put their wedding cards and gifts on; there were already 6 or 7 gifts on it, sent from people who were invited, who wouldn't be able to make it there for one reason or another.

Father Salva was there, of course, and after saying the daily Mass on Friday, offered to concelebrate the wedding Mass, as Father Jim would marry the young couple. Many friends who weren't Catholic would be coming, including all of the bride's family. They would be welcomed, but Cora had explained to them that they couldn't take part in receiving Communion.

Hans was still working on the Blocker ranch, but he wanted to show his good friendship for Andrew and Cora by giving them something he knew that they needed, a good sized dresser for the rest of their clothes. He didn't have time to make one himself, but he had met Dick York, who built furniture, and hired him to make a nice, full sized quality dresser. He had the dresser made of walnut wood, which was more expensive, but would last at least 50 years. Hans gave Dick York almost $13 just to pay for the wood, with the promise of paying $10 for the making of it. Dick then said that he had to have another man do the knobs on the drawers, and a metal sheet for the back of the dresser. He would need to pay him $2, and that wouldn't include the varnishing of the dresser. But Hans had been saving most of his money from his jobs, and had enough to give Dick the extra $2, plus 50 cents for the varnish. Dick didn't know Andrew very well, and wasn't invited to the wedding. But he said that he and his friend who did the knobs on the 6 drawers would take the dresser, when the varnish was dry, up to the bedroom in the house, with a handmade card with blessings on it from Hans. It would be a nice surprise for the newlyweds when they went to spend a first night together as Mr. and Mrs. Zerbee.

Saturday morning came, with no one eating breakfast so that they could take part in receiving holy communion at the 10 o'clock wedding Mass. Everyone who was Catholic wanted to be a part of this special Mass by receiving the Holy Eucharist, so they had to fast from midnight on. After the wedding they could eat at the reception in the Couper barn. Everyone who was invited, and a few who weren't, went to Good Shepherd Church, as early as 8:30 AM, to get a better seat behind the two front pews that were reserved for the bride and groom's family. Everyone was dressed in their own Sunday best, except for the bride, who would be wearing her mother's wedding dress. And the maid of honor, another bridesmaid, and the flower girl all wore a nice lavender Dress. Cora's maid of honor was a neighborhood friend, Cami Kutler, who was a member of Good Shepherd, and the bridesmaid was 14-year-old Elaine Ansara. Cora's 10-year-old sister was the flower girl. Andrew's best friend from school, Ed Ames, was his best man, and Robert Horton's 7-year-old son John was the ring bearer. The men all wore a dark suit of brown or blue. It didn't matter to them if they weren't the same color, as it did with the women's dresses. The men all wore a white shirt and a tie of some kind, they looked fine, even though they all had a different colored tie.

By 9:25 most of the people were in the church, almost as many as were there for Sunday Mass. Hans was in his Sunday outfit, and went to the second pew on the side for the groom to say a rosary for the bride and groom, before Mass. There were a few other family members, and a couple of friends in the second pew, with all of the bride's family in the front pew, except for the father, who would be walking his loving daughter down the aisle, to the front, where Hans and the wedding party were waiting. Andrew's family members knelt down in their front pew to say some prayers before Mass. The bride's family members noticed this, and also knelt, saying some prayers of their own. These Protestants were impressed with the beauty of Good Shepherd Church, as many of them were seeing the inside of a Catholic church for the first time. Stained glass windows, statues, and pictures of the stations of the cross were not things usually seen in a Protestant church.

At 9:45 the choir, made up of 16 people, sang a few songs before Mass, with some that the Protestants would be familiar with, like Faith of our Fathers, and one liked by both faiths, Amazing Grace. The bridal men and women were standing, with the groom, at the front of the church, as Father Jim and Father Salva came out to the altar, dressed in their nicest robes, after two altar boys lit the two candles on the altar. The last few people came in for the Mass, both invited and uninvited, as they filled in the last few pews left in the back of the church. As Father Jim and Father Salva were waiting to begin the Mass Father Jim said to Fr. Salva, "I felt bad when I had to tell Cora to let her family members know that they couldn't take part in communion, like the Catholics, but she understood, and did a good job of making her family understand that we weren't judging them, that it was just a Church rule we had to follow." Father Salva nodded, and said," Well, they're still with us as fellow Christians." "Maybe in the future Protestants will be able to receive, if they truly believe that Jesus is really in the Eucharist," said Father Jim. "But I don't think it will be in our time."

One of the altar boys then tugged at Father Jim's robe and said," It's almost 10 o'clock, Father." So both priests and both altar boys came out to the altar rail, as the pianist played Here comes the Bride. As Father Jim watched, Cora's father was walking his beautifully dressed daughter down the aisle, from the back of the church, until he reached the front, and gave his daughter a kiss, before leaving her with the groom. Father Jim then motioned for them to sit in the two chairs that had been set up, behind a small table, where they would remain until time for the ceremony.

So Father Jim and Father Salva went back to the altar and went on with the Mass, like on Sunday, except for just one reading, as in a daily Mass, which Father Salva said and then, after the responsorial, Father Jim read the Gospel from John: 15, 14 – 17. Then Father Jim gave a short homily about the sacred blessing of holy matrimony, and stepped forth, motioning to the bride and groom, and the rest of the wedding party to come forward.

Everyone in the church smiled, while a few cried, as some always do at this part of the wedding. Father Jim did his duty, having the happy couple go through their vows, before he proclaimed them man and wife. As Andrew kissed his bride Father Jim smiled and motioned for them to go back to their chairs in the middle of the aisle. Father Jim and Father Salva then went to the altar, and performed the Consecration of the bread and wine. When it came time for the people to receive the Holy Eucharist, Cora and Andrew came up first, receiving communion for the first time as man and wife. Then Andrew's family came up, then the rest of the Catholics in the church, with the choir singing Holy God, We Praise Thy Name. After communion Father Jim sat in his chair on the altar in reflection, then ended the Mass, as the bride and groom led the way to the back of the church, with the wedding party following, and then the family members, followed by the rest of the people, as a soprano sang O Promise me, until the bride and groom had left the church. After many greetings, hugs, and kisses, the new couple went with the others to the Couper barn in a car, or on a horse, if they didn't have a car or truck, for the reception. Most of the people knew where to go, the rest just followed the others. Five cooks who were in the back of the church left right after communion to start with the cooking of many good things that would be a welcome late breakfast for the Catholics who had gone to communion.

The Bride and groom led the way in an old surrey that had been decorated as nicely as could be with many paper streamers and bells, with two high stepping horses pulling it, as the groom's best man drove the team. Arriving at the barn, everyone went in and immediately went to the tables with their names on them, for the bride and the groom, the family members, and the wedding party. They all started to eat and drink, as the best man, then others, offered up a toast to the bride and groom. Then some men and women with fiddles, guitars, and other instruments played some popular songs, as Cora and Andrew danced for the first time as man and wife. Then Cora left Andrew to dance with her father, and the newlyweds took turns dancing with family members and friends. Cora was especially happy when Hans came to dance with her, and she danced with him longer than with any other person, except her husband. They had become good friends since she met Hans as he was working on the Zerbee farm, and then with Andrew to help build his new house, the one that Andrew and Cora would be living in. Of Course, Father Jim and Father Salva were there, & gave their blessings to the happy newlyweds, before the best man gave his last toast to the bride and groom, saying how it was God's way that they came to know each other, before falling in love. Then the newlyweds were ushered to the table with the nice wedding cake on it to cut it, and then to the table with many cards and almost 30 gifts, all nicely wrapped. While Cora and Andrew were opening some of the gifts, Hans told them that there was no gift from him there, but that they would get it later. They tried to get him to tell them what it was, but Hans just said, "No, it will be a surprise." Many of the townspeople were in the barn, including the mayor, the librarian, Postmaster Barnaby West, Jack Haley, the butcher, Clayton More, the sheriff, and others who congratulated the couple as they left the party, to go back to their place of business. The party ended at about 5 o'clock, and people went home to have supper, with the bride and groom accepting an invitation from Myra Quinn to have supper at her restaurant, for just the bride and groom and their parents. The younger children would be eating with other relatives. Then the newlyweds took the fancy horse drawn carriage and went to their new home, to spend their first night together as Mr. and Mrs. Zerbee.

Sunday morning was the same as any other Sunday, except for a dozen or so people who came for the wedding, and stayed overnight with family, or at the hotel. They came for Mass, before leaving for home, after a quick breakfast. Some had come in a car or truck, with a few riding a horse, or coming in a horse drawn wagon. One friend and his wife came from the upper part of the lower part of Michigan, two of the families came from the eastern part of the Upper Peninsula, three families came from Wisconsin, and one old friend who used to live in town came all the way from Minneapolis, Minnesota.

The church was almost full, with more than 20 visitors, plus the usual people from the parish. Father Jim gave a nice homily, mostly on the Holy family, as he was sure to welcome the church's newest family, who came to church together from the new home they lived in. Many people greeted the newlyweds again, with a few who congratulated them, who weren't able to make the wedding. When the newlyweds saw Father Jim, they said they wanted to pay him for marrying them. "No, it was my pleasure to see a couple like you get married in our church," said Father Jim.

After that, Cora and Andrew went to the back of the church to wait for Hans, who was still singing in the choir, just finishing up with the last verse of the song they had chosen for the recessional for the day. After they finished, the choir members separated, to go their own ways. Hans spotted Cora and Andrew, waving to him to come to them. As Hans got close to them Cora came up to Hans and kissed him on the cheek. "Oh, that is a wonderful gift," said Cora, as Andrew came up to him, and hugged him, and shook his hand. "You said your gift would be a surprise, and it was. We had all of our belongings already in the house, mostly in the downstairs, except for a few things, and what clothes we had taken from our two homes. Oh, thank you," said Cora again, as she kissed Hans on the other cheek. "You better behave yourself, you're a married lady now," kidded Hans. "You should have seen us," said Andrew. "it was our wedding night, but we spent more than a half hour examining our brand-new dresser, with a card on it wishing us a happy life together. We pulled out the drawers, and I told Cora what a nice piece of furniture it was, and that it was made of walnut, or some other quality wood." "It is walnut," said Hans, "I wanted nothing but the best for you and Cora. You'll still be using that when you're celebrating your 50th wedding anniversary." Then Andrew said,

"With Cora still in her wedding dress we spent the next half hour taking most of the clothes we had in the two boxes, and put them in the big drawers of our new, shiny dresser. Cora put her things on one side, I put mine on the other side. Then we took most of the clothes out of the smaller dresser that my father gave us, and nearly filled the dresser. We both have some clothes we left in our two parent's houses, now we can get them, we have room for all of them in the two dressers." "And the dresser looks so nice, and shiny," said Cora. "Yes, it is varnished,' said Hans. "Did you send away for it?" asked Andrew. "I've seen some dressers like it in a catalogue, but they didn't look this nice." "No, I had someone make it here," said Hans, I couldn't have made one this nice myself, I just bought the wood and gave someone something for putting it together." "We wanted to see you after Mass, to thank you," said Cora. "You should have seen us," said Andrew, "it wasn't until we had moved all the clothes into our best wedding gift that we realized that it was almost 10:30, and we were still in our wedding garb." "Yes, we then stopped looking at our wedding present, and…." Said Cora, as she looked coyly at Hans. "No explanation necessary," said Hans, "so, what do you two think of married life?" "Oh, it's wonderful," said Andrew and Cora, in unison. "Oh, there's some other people waiting to greet us,' said Andrew, we'll see them, then talk to you later." So Hans went to the rectory for a quick breakfast, before going back to the ranch, while the newlyweds received more congratulations, and two more wedding cards from friends who weren't at the wedding. Cora and Andrew then went to their new home, where Cora made a nice breakfast for her and her new, loving husband.

After their first breakfast as husband and wife Andrew took his horse to his father's house, to use the telephone to call the rectory, to leave a message for Hans. Marie answered the phone, and Andrew said, "Marie, I don't know if the Blockers have a telephone, I'd like to talk to Hans as soon as I can, it's about our Thanksgiving." "They do have a telephone," said Marie. "They just put it in last July, I'll give you the number, I think it's three longs and a short." "Thank you, "said Andrew, as Marie checked to make sure of the number. Then Andrew put in a call to the ranch, and Mrs. Blocker took Andrew's request for Hans to call his father's house when he got back in from the range.

Later Cora and Andrew were at the old Zerbee house as guests for the Zerbee supper. About a half hour after they finished supper the phone rang, it was Hans, who had just gotten back after a long day of moving cattle. "Hey Hans," said Andrew, "my parents are having a family get-together for our Thanksgiving dinner on Thursday; we want you to come, you're just like family." "Well, I think Dan will let me have the day off, since it's Thanksgiving,' said Hans, "thank you." "I was thinking of having our first Thanksgiving at my new house, but our table only is big enough for eight people. With Cora's parents, and Cora's brother and sister, we'll have 10, maybe 12 here, since we have also invited Father Jim and Marie, but I think they may have already been invited elsewhere," said Andrew. "That's good, when do you want me to be there," asked Hans. Andrew then asked his mother when dinner was. She took the telephone and said, "We'll be sitting down to eat at 2 o'clock, we'll just have a light breakfast earlier. Be here by then, and bring your appetite." "I will, and thank you," said Hans. "Oh, and my husband and I want to thank you for the nice dresser you gave to Andrew and Cora," said Mrs. Zerbee. "I haven't seen it yet, but I will the next time I go to their house. My Andrew took the clothes he had left here, he says he has room for them in the nice walnut dresser, or in the one we gave them."

So everyone got ready for the upcoming national holiday. Fr. Jim and Marie had already accepted an invitation for Thanksgiving with another parish family, and Father Salva had called to say he wouldn't be coming, as usual, as he had accepted an invitation from one of his parishioners, and that also, one of his elderly parishioners was very sick, could go to his final reward at any time, so he would stay at Saint John's for the weekend.

Thanksgiving Day came, and Mrs. Zerbee was busy with fixing a nice dinner, as the new Mrs. Zerbee joined her to help out, as did Cora's mother, when she got there, around 1 PM. So, the three women, and two of their daughters, had a nice dinner ready at 2 PM, while the men, who were talking about farming, and other things, came in for the feast. A small table had been set up for two of the small children, while the adults and older children sat at the big dining room table, as it would seat 10 people. Thanks was given to God for protecting all of their men in the service of their country, men who were with them for Thanksgiving at this time last year.

Andrew's parents gave a special thanks to Hans for the beautiful dresser he had given to Andrew and Cora. Cora's parents had been told about it, they were eager to see it sometime. "Yes," said Cora's mother, "I thought that the clothes Cora had to leave would be at our house for a while, but she had us bring them with us today for her, since she told us of the nice, larger dresser that she & Andrew have now, so they can have all of their clothes put neatly away.

Andrew's father played the part of the host as he carved the turkey, then let Andrew take over and finish the job. The 13–pound turkey's slices, and the two drumsticks were passed around, along with the dressing, mashed potatoes, rolls, cranberry sauce, sweet potatoes, peas, and other things that make a Thanksgiving dinner complete. Compliments were given to the cooks, of course, and Cora said that she would see about having their Thanksgiving dinner at their new house next year, that they would be all settled then, because now they had a lot of their gifts from their wedding still out, and that she still had to get busy with sending thank you notes to many people, even the ones who just sent a card. And, of course, many of the others there had questions for Andrew and Cora, as everyone wanted to know how they were adjusting to their new life as man and wife. Finally, Andrew's father stood up and said, "All right, we can ask Andrew and Cora some questions later, let's just let them eat their Thanksgiving dinner, as if this were any other Thanksgiving."

That was that, nothing else was said, except the usual "pass the gravy, or please pass the dressing." Everyone settled down and ate the nice dinner themselves, as some of them thought of some questions to ask them later, without getting too personal. This turned out to be the nicest Thanksgiving dinner ever held at the old Zerbee home.

Chapter 8

It was Sunday, the first Sunday of Advent. The choir in Good Shepherd Church was getting ready to sing the songs they had rehearsed more than one week ago, because there was no rehearsal on Thanksgiving. They sang 2 or 3 Christmas songs before the 9 AM Mass. Hans talked to Father Jim and said, "I don't see any Advent Wreath up by the podium." "No, it will be brought up in our procession from the rear of the church. It's how we begin Mass for the 4 Sundays of Advent, for the last two years," said Father Jim. "You see, 3 years ago one of our families asked if they could make the Advent Wreath themselves, with a member of their family lighting the candles for the four Sundays. The Hooper family was the first to do this the next year, as I reserved this new traditional doing for them. As our tradition started, the Gannor family asked if they could do it, and they did it, last year. This year the Prentice family has the honors. They came to me two years ago, two days after the Hooper family asked me; I told them they would have to wait until 1942. I already have a family that is signed up for next year, and before then I'll surely have at least one more of our families asking to take part in this, our own Good Shepherd Advent tradition. And the first two families have already told me that they would do it again, if I didn't have a family to do it. I don't think It will ever get back to them, unless it's years from now, when the next generation of the Hooper or Gannor families does it. There's even been some talk of making a nice wooden plaque to put on the wall of the church in the back, with a list of the years, and the family that did our Advent Wreath for that year. I think I'll do that, I'll ask one of our carpenters to do it, with the names of the first three families that did it, with room for 5 or 6 more families, for the coming years. It would be nice to show to visitors."

So, after the songs were sung before Mass, We Three Kings was sung as the procession started, for Mass. An altar boy came first, carrying the Crucifix, with one altar boy carrying two candles for the altar, then the Prentice family, as they carried the homemade Advent Wreath, covered with holly. After Harold and Maggie Prentice came six-year-old Edgar, five-year-old Gladys, three-year-old Susan, and one-year-old Aston, carried in his mother's arms. When they got to the front of the church Father Jim took the wreath from Harold and set it on a stand, near the podium, and just on the other side of the altar rail. Then the family sat in the 1st pew, which was reserved for the family, before an altar boy brought a taper he had just lit from one of the two candles on the altar, and handed it to Harold Prentice, who reached over the rail and lit one of the purple candles, for the first Sunday of Advent. Then Harold went back to the front pew with his family.

For the next three weeks the two older children, and then their mother would get their turn for lighting the candles. On Christmas the family would be back in some other pew, and an altar boy would light the Advent Wreath for the Christmas Mass. The church had a capacity of 278, it would be almost full on the Christmas and Easter celebration, with chairs brought in sometimes, in case they were needed.

Father Jim said the two first readings, then the Gospel from Luke that most of the people were familiar with. Then Father Jim gave his homily, a special one this year, because of the war. "As we begin the holy season of Advent," said Father Jim, with a solemn look on his face, "we must think of the many Americans who are not able to meet as we are now, because they are overseas preparing to fight for our nation, and its peace – loving people. At our first Sunday of Advent last year we didn't know then that in a few days we would be listening, as President Roosevelt addressed congress, and the nation, about the disastrous attack on Pearl Harbor by the Japanese. I think the best part of the President's talk was when he said that we would win the victory, so help us God. Our declaration of war on Japan still didn't directly involve us with a war against Germany, but when, a few days later, Germany declared war against the United States, we were officially involved with the war in Europe, also. We were then forced to defend ourselves against two nations that were threatening our freedom, and that of many other nations, as well.

Many of our young men were not even in the military at this time last year, but after Roosevelt's speech many men who recently graduated from high school, and two who were still in high school, signed up with our army or navy, and were off for basic training before Christmas of last year. And we must face the reality that we may never see some of them again. We can only pray for their safety, and do what we must here at home to support our fighting men. This is a topic not usually spoken of from a pulpit, but I think many other priests and ministers are also including this in their talk, especially the part about praying for the safety of our men. Now, we must remember that this is a joyous time of year, as we look forward to the celebration of Our Savior's birth, as Jesus was born of the Virgin Mary to free us from our sins. I want to thank our Ladies of Charity, and some of their husbands, for the nicely decorated Christmas trees on our altar, and for the poinsettias that grace our church.

Our choir, which is much larger than at this time last year is making our celebration much nicer, with the Christmas hymns that they will be singing for us during Advent, and the Christmas season. I also thank Harold and Maggie Prentice and their family, for supplying this year's Advent Wreath. It's heartwarming to see families who show their support for our parish by doing this, and other things that, I'm sure, will help build up treasure in Heaven, for doing God's work. I will be holding confessions on each Thursday, from1:30 to 3:30, as well as on Tuesday morning after the 8 AM Mass. Father Salva will also hear confessions on Saturday morning during Advent. In his absence, I will hear confessions Saturday, from 9 to 11 AM. And finally, I want to welcome Andrew and Cora Zerbee as they prepare to celebrate their first Christmas as man and wife. I heard that Cora has joined our Ladies of Charity, I know they will welcome her as they keep our church clean and in order, and who also get flowers for our altar at cost, or, on some occasions, donated by some of our gardeners. Oh, the Ladies of Charity will also be joining me for saying the rosary after daily Mass on Monday, and Friday. I'm glad to see some new faces, it's nice to have our church almost full. And, as you send out your Christmas cards, and do other things to prepare for getting together, always keep the spirit of Christmas in your heart."

Father Jim then went to his chair near the altar for a few minutes, while the congregation thought about the things Father had said in his homily. Then it was time for collection, as the altar boys helped Father Jim with setting things up on the altar, in preparation for the Consecration. With more people in the church, and with the Christmas spirit in their hearts, the people put a little more than usual in the collection baskets. After Mass Father Jim noticed that some of the people who had been helped by the fundraiser had put, their envelope, as much as a dollar in for collection, people who usually only gave a little change, or nothing. They had evidently saved a little of the money they had been given, to support their church, as their church had supported them.

The choir sang Silent Night for communion, as they would again each week for the Advent and Christmas Masses. Then O Little Town of Bethlehem sounded a little better than ever, with the 24 – member choir, as the people left the church with many smiles and good wishes to friends, and to some people that they didn't see in church every week. Several people greeted Father Jim and told him how much they liked his homily, including some of the ones who didn't make it to Mass evert Sunday, mostly because of where they lived, outside the town, or for one other reason, like sickness in the family. Some others also greeted Andrew & Cora, and congratulated them on their marriage. The newlyweds received 3 more wedding cards, and some asked them what their new address was, as they would like to send them a Christmas card for their first Christmas together. Andrew told them that it is the same as his father's address, as they live on his farm, a little way to the back part of it.

People also complimented the choir, they noticed the difference it made with 24 voices, instead of the 11 they had last year. A farmer named Ronald Ragan told them that they should sing on the radio. And a waitress named Phyllis Thaxter said that she didn't always make it to Mass, but that she wouldn't miss it, and the hearing of the beautiful singing. "It was Hans who helped get us more new singers," said Chester Good, the choir leader. "But I didn't get all the new singers," said Hans, who had overheard Chester. "So, you're Hans, who got some more of the singers we have now?" asked Phyllis, "I don't know your last name." "It's Kruger," said Hans. "This is Phyllis Thaxter," said Chester. "I know her from school, she and I and Andrew Zerbee graduated last June, along with Cora Ryan, er, I mean Zerbee, it's hard to remember her married name, sometimes." "And, as I said, I'll make it to Sunday Mass from now on," promised Phyllis. "I work late Saturday night, I don't always wake up in time to make it to 9 AM Mass on Sunday, though my parents do. But I'll be sure to get up on time, and not miss Mass from now on. And did you also graduate in our class, Hans?" "No," said Hans, "I graduated the year before, from a school a long way from here; I'm working on the Blocker ranch now." "Oh, I'm the waitress at the Turner Diner, run by Abagail Turner. I sometimes do some of the cooking, also. I'm a good cook." "Oh, is that the one on Maple Street?" asked the choir leader. "Yes," said Phyllis, "I started working there two weeks after I was done with school." "Well, it's nice to meet you," said Hans, "see you in church on Sunday?" "Yes, and I might make it to daily Mass on Friday, that's my day off," said Phyllis.

So Hans went over to the rectory for breakfast. He told father Jim that he had a couple of compliments for the songs the choir sang, after Mass, one of the women who was in the same class as Andrew and Cora Zerbee. Her name is, uh, Phyllis . . . Thaster." "Do you mean Thaxter?" asked Father Jim. "Oh yes, do you know her?" asked Hans. "I've known the Thaxter family some, since they moved to Cross Bear last January, when they came to the rectory to join the parish. They used to live in the eastern part of the peninsula, a little way from Heeawatha, so they went to Mass at St. John's. But when I was talking with Father Salva about 3 weeks ago he told me that they didn't make it to Mass every Sunday," said Father Jim. "Is Phyllis the only child?" asked Hans. "No," said Father Jim, "they have three children, older than Phyllis, two sons and a daughter. They are still back in a little town near Heeawatha. The older ones, Jake and Laurie, are married, and I heard that the younger son Josh is planning on getting married in January. Her older brother and sister have been married for about two years, they both have one child." "So, Phyllis is an aunt," said Hans. "Yes, but the family isn't very strong in the Faith," said Father Jim. "The older son married a Protestant woman, but Father Salva had her sign the papers that she promised to raise any children Catholic.

As for her sister, she married a Catholic, but Josh will also be marrying a Protestant woman, who won't sign the papers for raising the children Catholic, so they won't be married in a Catholic Church. I've noticed that Phyllis seems to enjoy going to Mass. I've seen her stay in the pew and pray after her parents had left the pew. One time I saw her go to our votive candles, and put a dime in the box before lighting a votive candle, and saying a prayer, before her father came to get her, and take her home. The women seem to be the better Catholics in their family." "Phyllis told me that she would be here for Mass every Sunday from now on,' said Hans," She says she wants to hear our singing, but I think she really wants to come for our weekly celebration, not just for the music." Father Jim nodded in agreement.

On Tuesday Hans came to town with Dan Blocker to help with getting some supplies for the ranch, from a general store on Maple Street, about a block away from the diner where Phyllis Thaxter worked. Hans asked if he could go to the diner that Phyllis works in for a few minutes. Dan said to go ahead, he would be at the store for at least a half hour to get the items to put in his truck. So Hans went down the street to the diner, and as he went in the door he saw Phyllis clearing off some tables, getting the dishes left from people who had been there for breakfast. "Oh Hans," said Phyllis, as she saw Hans coming towards her, "just give me a minute, I just have this last table to take care of." As she took a tray of dirty dishes to the kitchen a woman stepped out of the kitchen. "Oh, Abagail," said Phyllis, this is my friend from church, Hans Kruber, he sings in the choir." "Well, I'm pleased to meet you," said Abagail, "I've heard of you, and the nice choir you have." "Oh yes," said Hans, I, and Phyllis, go to Good Shepherd Church. I would like to talk to Phyllis, if she has a moment." "Oh, sit down and have a cup of coffee," said the owner of the diner. Phyllis has had a busy morning; she can take a break." "I'll get the coffee," said Phyllis." "I just came in from the field, I don't have any cash on me," said Hans. "It's on the house," said Abagail, and have some of those nice doughnuts, too. There's some glazed ones." "I never had a glazed doughnut," said Hans." "Well, help yourself. I'll get the dishes ready for washing," said Abagail to Phyllis. "All right, thank you," said Hans.

So Hans and Phyllis sat down at a table, with a cup of coffee, and some nice glazed doughnuts that were just baked that morning. "I can only stay a few minutes," said Hans, "I have to get back to help Mr. Blocker bring some things he is getting now, back to the ranch. I was talking to Father Jim, he said that he has known your family pretty well, since you came here in January. I know about your two brothers and sister who didn't come with you when you came here last January. I told Father that you would be coming to Mass every Sunday." "Yes, I want to hear you and the others in choir sing again." "But I have a feeling that you want to come for the Mass, too, am I right?" asked Hans. "Yes, but I don't know if I can make it on Friday. I don't have a car, and our house is several blocks on the other side of the diner. My father takes the car to go to work every Friday morning,' said Phyllis." "I thought there might be a transportation problem," said Hans, it's what, about 7 blocks from here to Good Shepherd?" "Yes, and my parents live another 3 blocks the other way, it's a little over 10 blocks." said Phyllis. "You know our mayor, don't you?" asked Hans. After Phyllis nodded yes, Hans said: "I know that the mayor comes to daily Mass almost every day, he'll surely make it every day during Advent, give me your address. He lives in the house behind the town hall, he'll be glad to pick you up on Friday morning, probably around 7:20 or so. He'll probably have his wife with him, the kids will be in school." "Oh, that would be wonderful!" said Phyllis, are you sure he won't mind?" "No, he's a good friend, he'll be happy to do it," and bring you home after, as well," said Hans. "And on Friday they'll be saying the rosary after Mass," said Hans. "Yes, I remember hearing Father O'Connell saying that in church, maybe it will give me a chance to get to know some more of the Ladies of Charity, as well, since we will be helping to lead the rosary," said Phyllis. "I don't know if it will be Father Salva, or Father O'Connell who will say the Mass. Father Salva might be too busy with his duties at St. John's to visit us for two days a week, during our Advent season," said Hans. "I haven't seen him since we moved here," said Phyllis, it would be nice to see him again." "Well, I'll tell the mayor to pick you up about 7:15, I know he likes to get there early enough for some private prayers, or once In a while, the rosary. Of course, you'll be saying that after Mass," said Hans. "But now I must finish this good cup of coffee, and this delicious doughnut, and get back to Dan so we can get back to the ranch." Hans took a last sip of coffee, and thanked Phyllis for the nice talk, and left the diner, with a smiling waitress escorting him to the door, just as the first person for an early lunch came in. It was time for the smiling young waitress to get back to work, also.

The first week of Advent went by, with the choir meeting on Thursday night for their rehearsal, to practice the regular songs for this Sunday, and also some of the ones they would be singing for the Bishop, when he came, the following week, for the Third Sunday of Advent. Friday morning the mayor and his wife did stop at the Thaxter home, and picked up Phyllis to take her to morning Mass. She was very grateful, and joined in with Father Jim and the other Ladies of Charity who were at the Mass to help lead with the rosary. She met five of them for the first time, as they all welcomed her into their devoted church group. Phyllis then went back with Robert Horton and his wife to the town hall, so that Phyllis could go window shopping, before going back to her home, and having a late breakfast. Robert had asked Phyllis' mother if she also wanted to go to Mass. But she said that she had a lot of housework to do, but that she would be there Sunday.

The Second Sunday of Advent came, and six year old Edgar Prentice did the job of getting the lit taper from the altar boy, & leaning over the altar rail to light, first, the purple candle that had been lit last week, then another purple candle, for the Second week of Advent. By now the choir was singing all Christmas carols for Mass, with two or three before Mass, as well. Father Jim gave another inspiring homily, on the true meaning of Christmas, and reminded everyone that the Bishop would be here next week. More parishioners came to Mass during Advent, but even more would come to see the Bishop, since many of them had never seen him in person. Phyllis Thaxter came again for Mass on the Friday before the 3rd Sunday of Advent, with her mother this time. The mayor and his wife told Phyllis and her mother about the Bishop, since they had met him when he was there, about three years ago.

Saturday came, and about 6 o'clock a car came with Bishop Matthew H. Clarke, S. J. in his 1940 Studebaker, which was a very nice car then. A stranger was driving, and the Bishop introduced Father Jim to Jason A. Hogan, who was in his third year in the seminary. He had been sent to assist the Bishop during Advent, to gain some of the parochial experience that a priest would need to know.

"Welcome to Good Shepherd," said Father Jim, as he kissed the Bishop's ring. "That's a pretty nice car you have." "Yes," said Bishop Clarke, "we were able to get it two years ago, by selling a bond we had been saving for just that purpose. We would not be able to get a car like it today, as things are tight since Pearl Harbor. There are not many cars even available for the average citizen, since the automakers are now making a lot of jeeps, planes, tanks, and other things for our military forces. One of my people is good with cars, he says he'll keep it running good for me, no matter how old it gets." Bishop Clarke and his seminarian ate with Father Jim, as Marie had put up a late supper for her old friend; she remembered the Bishop when he was here for his last visit.

The Third Sunday of Advent was a busy morning, with the choir getting ready for Mass, with many people coming to see their Bishop. As the first half hour before Mass passed until 9 AM, the choir sang some Christmas songs, as the Bishop, his young seminarian, Father Jim, and two altar boys all waited for the clock to strike nine. Then their procession started, with the altar boys first, then the seminarian, then Father Jim, then the Bishop, in his best regalia, came out on the altar. As the clergy went to the altar, one of the altar boys got a taper to light from one of the candles. The Bishop didn't know about their Advent Wreath tradition, and he looked on with interest as five-year-old Gladys Prentice came out of the front pew, took the taper from the altar boy, then leaned over the rail and lit the two purple candles that were lit last week, and then the pink candle, for the Third Week of Advent. She then gave the taper back to the altar boy who blew it out, and put it over by the side of the altar. Then the girl went back to the front pew, smiling up at the Bishop, and waving at him. The Bishop slowly returned her wave, as the girl got back in the pew with her family. The

Bishop turned toward Father Jim with a blank look on his face, and Father Jim told him he would tell him about what he had just seen, later. The choir was just finishing with their opening song, and many were there to hear the new choir for the first time. The pews were full, while twenty or more people stood In the back of the church. Father Jim said to Bishop Clarke, "We don't usually have a packed church, except on Christmas and Easter. A lot of people came just to see you, your Eminence."

The Mass then continued on, as Father Jim concelebrated with the Bishop, as the seminarian assisted, along with the altar boys. The Bishop gave the homily. He said how glad he was to be here, and the usual talk about the meaning of Christmas. He told of some of the things going on at the cathedral, and some news he had received from the dioceses in the lower part of Michigan. He got the attention of the people when he told of a letter he received from Pope Pius XII, just as Advent started. "Our Pope," said the Bishop, "told of a lot of concern for what was going on around Rome with what the Nazis were doing to find any Jews, or sometimes Catholics, and arresting them, as many were fleeing from Italy, in occupied France, parts of Germany, and in occupied Poland." The people nodded, they had already been praying for these unfortunate people. Then the Bishop said: "I've been a priest for 28 years, a bishop for 11 years, but I have never before seen a sweet, innocent child come up and light the Advent Wreath. I will ask Father O'Connell about it, It's very interesting to me. As he said this, a little girl in the front pew smiled, and looked up at her mother, as her mother hugged her sweet and Innocent girl. Then the Bishop said some closing words, and finished with a blessing for all of the people. The rest of the Mass went smoothly, and Father Jim noticed how many people put something in for the collection. The parishioners were giving their usual gift for Sunday Mass, with a few giving more, because of the presence of the Bishop. For the communion the Bishop and Father Jim both gave out the holy Eucharist in the front part of the church, while the seminarian was given 25 hosts to take to the choir, and to the pianist, before they started singing Silent Night. After finishing with communion Father Jim and the Bishop went back to the chairs on the side of the altar. The Bishop then said to Father Jim, "We usually wait until a seminarian is about to take his vows before they are allowed to give out communion, but Jason shows great promise for the priesthood, he's already deeper into his theological studies than the others. So I gave him permission to give out communion to your choir members."

Father Jim had found out through friends that Immaculate Mary was the Bishop's favorite song. So, as Mass ended, the choir sang Immaculate Mary instead of the usual Christmas song, for the recessional. For the second verse, Frankie Lane, their best tenor, sang it solo, until the rest of the choir joined in with "Ave, Ave, Ave Maria…." Their best soprano, Barbara Eller, sang the third verse as a solo, with the rest of the choir joining in, again, for the refrain. They sang the 4th verse together, then sang the first verse again, as the Bishop was still greeting people in the back of the church before he and Father Jim, and the seminarian, went back up to the sacristy, to take off their robes. The choir was still singing more Christmas carols until the Bishop left the church, to make their music resonate for the people who were still in the pews, saying some private prayers. But, as the Bishop walked by the choir he thanked them for singing Immaculate Mary, while some of them said how glad they were to meet him, and asked for his prayers, especially if they had a sick family member at home, or a son overseas.

As Bishop Clarke, Father Jim, and the seminarian enrobed, the Bishop gave a sincere thank you for the choir. "I didn't really expect to hear Immaculate Mary at an Advent Mass," said the Bishop, as he handed his robe to the seminarian. "And your choir, though fewer in number, sounds as nice as any choir I've ever heard." "Our choir members will be glad to hear that," said Father Jim. Then the Bishop, and the seminarian, listened intently as Father Jim explained about their tradition with one of their families providing, and lighting, the Advent Wreath, works. He told them of how happy the families are to do it, and that he already has two families lined up for the next two years, and that he'll wait until next year before accepting an offer from one of their other fine, upstanding families. He also told of how he only accepts the families with 2 or more children aged 5 or older. This makes it a real family deal, as the children also become a part of the special tradition.

As the Bishop sat down for a nice breakfast in the rectory Bishop Clarke said, "I'm going to tell about your family Advent Wreath tradition at my next meeting. I'm sure I'll have people wanting to do it for the cathedral, as well." "I'm sure you'll have families scheduled for the next 3 years, after you tell of it," said Father Jim, "but you will probably want to hold off on signing families up too far ahead of time, they might not be in a position to do it 4 years from now. I just have 2 families lined up, I'll get a new one each year." Then Father Jim went back to the church for a special 2 o'clock to 3 o'clock hour of confessions, since he didn't have time for all of the people on Saturday. The Bishop offered to go and hear confessions, also, so he sat in one confessional, with Father Jim in the other. Most of the people went to the Bishop, of course. Then it was time to go to the mayor's house, and the Zerbee farm, where the Bishop was taken to the newlywed's new house, where he gave a blessing on their home, and for a long and happy marriage. Cora and Andrew wouldn't let the Bishop go until they ushered him & the seminarian, upstairs, to show off their nice new dresser.

Then it was time for the bishop to return to Marquette. Bishop Clarke thanked Father Jim, Marie, and finally, their choir. The Studebaker left the rectory at 5 PM, with the Bishop, and the future Rev. Jason A. Hogan, who told Father Jim that he would send him a Christmas card, and tell him of his studies.

Everything was pretty much "back to normal" after that, as everyone was getting ready for Christmas, with Christmas trees, outside and inside decorations, last minute Christmas shopping, and plans for hosting, or going to, a Christmas dinner. Soon the choir went to their last rehearsal for the Fourth Sunday of Advent, and the Christmas Mass. As the Fourth Sunday of Christmas came, the choir sang Christmas songs, but different ones than they had planned for Christmas. Mrs. Prentice went up and lit up all four of the candles on the Advent Wreath. They were now done with their job with the Wreath, for this year. The church wasn't packed, as it was a week ago, with their Bishop being there, but it was still pretty full. A few of the people went to the Prentice family as they left the church, as they thanked them for doing the Advent Wreath, and mentioning how nice their 5 year old Gladys looked when she lit the candles, and then waved to the Bishop, with the Bishop waving back. "It's a nice looking Advent Wreath," said a friend. "It's the Prentice Advent Wreath" said 5 year old Gladys Prentice.

From then on everyone was just getting ready for Christmas, taking care of some last minute things, receiving some last Christmas cards to put up with their others on their mantle, or on the wall, or somewhere, to add to their Christmas décor. Some were getting ready to go to a relative's house out of town, while others were getting things all set for the Christmas dinner they would be having for their family, and others. People were all wishing others a Merry Christmas, as some would say, in reply, "We'll see you in church." Everyone in the churches in Cross Bear loved the Christmas season.

Chapter 9

The days were going by fast, but there was time to get some last minute things done, since Christmas came on a Friday this year. The Bishop had already sent word to the churches in the Diocese that he had granted absolution for the people to eat meat on Friday, so they could have a turkey, or chicken, or other meat for their Christmas dinner, so it wouldn't be a sin to eat meat on this one Friday, since it was Christmas.

"Yes, the Bishop left us his letter before he left last week," said Father Jim, to Marie, "he says the celebration of Christmas is more important than a Church ruling, like not eating meat on Friday." "That must have been a relief for many, since the ladies are so used to having meat for the Christmas dinner," said Marie. "As early as two weeks ago I got a question from one of the ladies about having a way around fixing their usual turkey dinner," said Father Jim, "I just told her that I couldn't give permission, but that I expected the Bishop would give us his dispensation." "Yes, when I saw you tell the people after Mass last Sunday about it," said Marie, "I saw a lot of people smiling, in the congregation. Do you think that other bishops are giving dispensation, also?" "I am sure they are, most of them, at least," said Father Jim. "O," said Marie, "I got the word that Andrew and Cora Zerbee will be having a Christmas dinner in their place, just for the immediate family. They didn't have enough room for Thanksgiving, but they have enough room for just a few people, their parents and children. Cora's parents are having their own dinner, at their house, with some friends. They also invited Hans to the dinner, always room for one more, I guess. But Hans has already accepted an invitation to the Blocker family's dinner. Hans also called me from the ranch yesterday, asking me if it would be all right to get Phyllis Thaxter a Christmas present. He says he thinks she's a nice girl, she's got her parents coming back to Mass regularly." "What did you say to him?" asked Father Jim. "Well, I suggested a nice dress," said Marie, "but he said that he didn't even know if she would want one, or what color or style she would like, and he didn't know what size to get." "But of course," said Father Jim, "he shouldn't get her a dress, or any clothes; Hans must have enough sense for giving that kind of a gift." "I just told him to get her a nice gift, like, maybe a music box or something," said Marie, "and maybe a nice box of chocolates. I think Hans likes Phyllis." "Well, she is a pretty girl, but Hans is so religious, I think he likes her because she is a very good Catholic," said Father Jim, "Oh, it's December 23rd, just two more days until our wonderful celebration. I know the choir will give us a nicer Mass than we have had before, because of the 24 singers who do such a good job with our old, and newer Christmas hymns. Chester Good told me that they will be getting to the church about 8:30, and sing for about 25 minutes, before singing their regular songs for the Mass..." "I'm sure it will be nice," said Marie, "last year we only had eleven singers, and the 3 men were drowned out by the eight women."

It snowed Wednesday night, until about 11 o'clock in the morning. They got about 4 inches of snow, they would have a white Christmas. At the Blocker ranch Dan had arranged for one man to look after the cattle, which would be put in a corral, so that Hans could go where he wanted on the day before Christmas, with a horse, as he would be visiting the rectory, and stopping at the Turner Diner to drop off two packages for Phyllis Thaxter, which she was made to promise not to open until Christmas. He had gotten her a nice box of chocolates, which were a little more expensive now, because of the sugar shortage, and another item that he thought she would like. Phyllis was surprised, as she said that she didn't get him anything. "I'm just so happy that your family is going to Mass again," said Hans, maybe you can join me for welcoming the new year in." "Oh yes, and I'll try to join you for Christmas, I'll open the gifts before coming to Mass," said Phyllis. As Christmas came, Marie asked Father Jim about some churches she had heard of that had a Mass at midnight for Christmas. "Yes, I know that many other churches do that," said Father Jim, I'm going to ask around after Christmas, if enough parishioners want it, I'll have a Midnight Mass next year."

With Christmas morning many people were waking, and getting dressed in their best outfits before coming to church, some came more than a half hour early to say private prayers, say the rosary, or just to get a good seat, since they knew that the church would be packed. They again looked at all the Christmas decorations, and noticed who else came to church, some of whom were good friends. The choir members were all there at 8:30, and were getting ready for singing. But just then Phyllis Thaxter, who had opened the gifts Hans had given to her, came to Hans and pulled him aside. "Oh, thank you so much for the nice jewelry box," said Phyllis, "I don't have much jewelry, just a watch my mother gave me, and a few earrings, and a necklace. I had just been keeping them in a drawer, but now I have a nice place to put them. I wish I had known, I should have gotten you something." "Just sharing some of Christmas with me will be fine," said Hans. "After I have dinner at the ranch, Dan said I could take his truck to visit Andrew and Cora Zerbee. I can stop and pick you up first, you can come with me, I'm sure Andrew and Cora will be glad to see you." "That will be nice," said Phyllis, "we'll probably be finished with dinner by 3 o'clock." "I'll get there a little after 3," said Hans. Phyllis nodded, then leaned forward and kissed Hans on the cheek. "Hey, Romeo," said Chester Good, we're ready to start singing." So Hans left Phyllis, as she went to sit with her parents.

The choir started their songs with O Little Town of Bethlehem, then with It came Upon a Midnight Clear, then O Holy Night, then

We Three Kings of Orient Are, then O Come, O Come Emmanuel, until it was time for Mass. The people who came early really enjoyed the nice Christmas songs, sung by 24 voices, mostly in four part harmony. As the two altar boys and Father Jim came in from the back of the church the choir sang Adeste Fideles to start the celebration. After Father Jim and the altar boys were on the altar, the pianist kept playing until one of the altar boys lit the Advent Wreath. The Pritchard family was in a pew they usually sit in, their job was done, and the first pew was reserved for people who walked with a cane, so that they wouldn't have to go far for receiving communion. Mass moved along, and soon Father was at the podium reading the first two readings, and the familiar reading from Luke, Chapter 2, verses 1 through 7.

Then the people sat down for the homily, except for about 30 people who were standing, on the sides, or the back of the church. The ushers had brought up about 20 chairs from the basement, but there was still standing room only for the rest, as there was every Christmas, and Easter. Father Jim looked out at the sea of expectant faces, some of whom he saw only twice a year, and began to talk.

"It is always so nice to see the church so full of our faithful," said Father Jim. "We are here to worship Our Lord, to celebrate His birth, and to give thanks for the many blessings we still have, despite the hard times some of us have because of our sickness, and of some who have seen their sons, or brothers, or fathers leave us to fight for our country. Their families have received letters from them, while they are in boot camp, and some more saying that they will be going overseas soon, and that they might not be able to write for a while. Their families, and some friends, have sent them a Christmas card, and since I have received their last address, we have sent them a Christmas card from Good Shepherd, telling them that we're behind all of them, and that we will be praying for them. I've preached to you all, privately, of the seriousness of war. About a year ago a man visited me, and told me that there are two rules in war. Rule number 1 is, young men die, and rule number 2 is, you can't change rule number 1. The names of the men from our area have been put up in the town hall. We still have some sick members, one of whom is John Wane, he's 94. He took sick yesterday, and Elsie Borden, a nurse, is with him for now. We thank our Ladies of Charity for our nicely decorated church, and our choir is giving us beautiful music, nicer than we've ever had since Good Shepherd was built, with the 24 singers we now have. The Bishop was impressed with our choir. I thank all who invited Marie and myself for Christmas dinner. The first request was from one of our young couples, Gannor and Janice Rule. They have a son Nolan, who is one and a half years old, and Janice has another baby on the way. Going back to the war, we must realize that it won't be over soon, we have many countries to liberate from the enemy, many countries to free in Europe, and also in the Pacific theater. We must pray for the safety of our men. But for now, we celebrate the coming of the Messiah, because of what he would do to save us from our sins. We know of what Jesus did, from our Scriptures, and we also hear of the special role Mary played in the coming of Jesus, as she said to the angel: Be it done to me, according to thy word. Of course, we hear a lot about the things Jesus did during his ministry as He preached to the people, cured the sick, even raised some from the dead, as He did with His friend Lazarus. And though Jesus was divine, He also showed that He was human when, upon hearing of Lazarus' death, he wept. But one person we don't hear much about is Joseph. He stood with Mary when Jesus was born, then took Mary and Jesus into Egypt to escape the wrath of Herod. Upon returning to Nazareth he did the part of a father as he helped raise Jesus, and looked after Mary. Nothing much is said about Joseph in Scripture. The last we hear of him was when he and Mary returned to the Temple to find 12 year old Jesus talking to the elders, and asking them questions. We find nothing written about Joseph after that, but he was still a part of God's plan, and he doesn't get much credit. So, as you celebrate this wonderful Christmas day in your home, or someone else's, remember your loved ones, remember Jesus, but also find it in your heart to remember Joseph."

Father Jim then went over to his chair near the altar, as the congregation sat in silence as they thought about what Father Jim's homily. Then Father Jim went to the podium for the petitions, as their old sick parishioner was mentioned, and all of their men who were away serving their country. Then the altar boys started getting things ready for the consecration, as collection was taken up, as the choir sang O Little Town of Bethlehem, with some people putting in more money than usual for Christmas, as was the usual thing for Christmas Mass. Some put as much as $5 in the collection, with one person putting in $10. There were more people to give money, and Father Jim saw a few people who had been helped with the fundraiser putting in as much as a dollar. They were still supporting their church, even if they didn't have as much to give as the rest of the congregation.

Father Jim then consecrated the bread and wine, and quickly brought over holy communion to the choir and pianist, before going back to the front to give communion to the rest of the people, as all but a few people came to receive the Body of Christ, on this special day. Father Jim first went to the front pews, with an altar boy holding the paten, to give communion to those in the front who would have difficulty walking up to receive. Then he went to his place behind the altar rail to take care of the rest of the people coming up to receive. By then the choir started singing Silent Night, and they did it in the same way they sang immaculate Mary for the Bishop. After singing the 1st verse in four part harmony, their best tenor again sang solo, the 2nd verse, then their soprano sang the 3rd verse, with the whole choir finishing with the 4th verse. With some people still coming up for communion, the pianist played two more verses of Silent Night, until the last of the people were back in their seats. As the altar boys cleared the altar, and then went to sit in chairs by Father, Father Jim noticed that 5 or 6 people in the back of the church had left, after receiving communion. The Mass had taken more than an hour and a half, it took about 20 minutes for everyone to receive communion. Usually no one left after communion, they waited until the priest left the altar. Before leaving the altar, Father Jim told everyone to remember all our loved ones in their prayers, and to keep the spirit of Christmas in their hearts always. Father Jim and the altar boys processed to the back of the church, as the choir loudly sang Joy to the World, in 4-part harmony. They had saved this song for Christmas, they didn't sing it during Advent. Then they sang We three Kings, as some people were still in church looking at the decorated church, or Just saying some private prayers. But most of the people had left by then, to get home for a late breakfast, and to start preparing for their Christmas dinner, unless they were waiting to travel to another person's home for dinner there.

Father Jim and Marie went to the rectory for breakfast, also. "I'm surprised you could get way so soon," said Marie, there were so many people congratulating you for your homily. And then you had to go and take care of your robe, and make sure that the altar boys did their job, before thanking them, and wishing them a Merry Christmas. And then you came through the church and greeted some more people who had been there after the Mass to say some private prayers.

As Father Jim sat down to eat a late breakfast, it was about 11 o'clock. "That was a lovely Christmas homily you said," said Marie, I saw many of our parishioners talking to you, they didn't just say Merry Christmas, did they?" "No, many of them said nice things about the homily, saying that they would remember Joseph," said Father Jim. "Of course, they wished me a Merry Christmas, as well, as three of them handed me a Christmas card." "I think we have more Christmas cards on display here in the rectory than we ever had," said Marie. "And with the cards we sent to our servicemen, we sent more cards than ever before, also," said Father Jim" "We didn't send a card to all the parishioners, but we still mailed out more than 70 cards," said Marie, we'll have to get more cards, we only have about 40 or so left for next year."

After breakfast Marie and Father Jim relaxed for a while, and listened to Carols on the radio, looked at all the Christmas cards they had received, before Father Jim got down at the table and counted the large Christmas collection. "We'll have enough for paying our bills, and about $70 for our petty cash fund," said Father Jim, "there will be more money for our parishioners who will need help for something, we'll have enough to give at least $5 to each of the ones who are in need."

Later Father Jim and Marie went to the Rule house, where Gannor and Janice were waiting for them. Mrs. Rule had cooked a nice chicken dinner, since a chicken dinner was enough for the four of them, as Nolan was still on baby food. "We're so happy to have you with us," said Janice, "maybe you can come again sometime in the future, when our two children are big enough to eat at the table with us." "We'll see," said Father Jim, "but that won't be for a while, since your second bundle from Heaven won't be here until March." Father Jim then gave his blessing for the nice meal, and enjoyed the nice dinner Janice had fixed.

Everywhere in town, and on some farms and ranches, people were enjoying a nice Christmas dinner. All the presents were opened, except for some that were taken with some who were going to another house for dinner, to be with relatives or friends to celebrate Christmas, and, of course, to compliment the cook.

After a nice dinner at the Blocker ranch, Hans was given the keys to Dan Blocker's truck. Hans drove into town, and went to the Thaxter home to pick up Phyllis Thaxter. As he parked the truck he saw Phyllis on the front porch, wearing a nice dress, the one she had worn to church. "Did you have a nice dinner?" asked Hans. "Oh. Yes, my mother and I fixed a nice roast beef dinner, for something different," said Phyllis, "and I have a gift for you," she said as she handed him a nicely wrapped package. "I felt guilty when you gave me those nice presents," said Phyllis, I still have some chocolates saved for you." Then Hans opened up the package. "Why, it's a nice sweater," said Hans. "Yes, I started to knit it back before we moved here from Green River," said Phyllis, "I was thinking of maybe doing it for my father, but after we came here a neighbor gave us some clothes, as we had traveled light as we started our new life here. My father was given a nice sweater, since it was January, so he didn't need the one I was making. So I just kept it, and then I remembered that I hadn't seen you wearing a sweater." "No, I have a warm jacket, but no sweater,' said Hans. And a nice sweater will be more comfortable, and it will be extra nice, because you made it," said Hans, as he gave Phyllis a hug. He thought about kissing her on the cheek, as Cora had done with him in church, but didn't, as they slowly parted. But then she leaned forward and kissed him on the lips. "You're supposed to kiss, under the mistletoe, at this time of year," said Phyllis. Hans nodded, then looked up and saw no mistletoe over them. He then looked at Phyllis as she smiled up at him. "Oh, you're a sneaky woman," said Hans. Phyllis leaned forward and gave him another quick kiss, then said, "Why don't you take off your jacket, and put your new sweater on. It's cold, you might need your jacket on, over it, as well,' said Phyllis. Hans nodded, and took his jacket off as Phyllis held the sweater for him to put on. "Oh, it's so comfortable, and warm," said Hans, "but I'll still put my jacket on over it, I won't have to zip it up, with the nice warm sweater." "we had better go," said Hans, Cora and Andrew will be waiting for me." So they got in the truck, and Hans drove to the Zerbee farm, where they made a quick stop at the main house, to say some more Merry Christmases, before going on to the house of Andrew and Cora.

Hans and Phyllis were welcomed in, just as Cora was putting away the clean and dried dishes from their Christmas meal. "Oh, I love your house," said Phyllis, to Cora. "Thanks," said Cora, "my husband and Hans built it." "Well, I just did some of it," said Hans, "Andrew did most of it." "You're too modest," said Andrew, "I wouldn't have had It finished in time for the wedding without Hans." They then sat down at the table where eight people were sitting about two hours ago. They talked about Christmas, their nice dinner, and Father Jim's homily. Hans showed off his nice new sweater, and Cora asked Phyllis how to do that kind of stitch, before taking Phyllis upstairs to show her their nice new dresser, that was their nicest wedding gift.

Hans and Phyllis then left, and Hans took Phyllis back to her home, and then took Dan Blocker's truck back to the ranch. Ordinarily Hans would have taken advantage for being in town with the truck, to do some shopping, for himself, or for things to pick up for Dan Blocker. But all the stores were closed, of course, it was Christmas.

Back at the rectory Marie and Father Jim had returned, after their nice Christmas dinner with Gannor and Janice Rule, and their young son. They sat back on the couch and relaxed for a while as they again listened to Christmas carols on the radio. Then the phone rang, and Father Jim answered it. After a few "I see," and "all rights", Father Jim hung up the phone. "Someone calling us to wish us a Merry Christmas?" asked Marie. "No, it's the nurse who has been looking after our 94-year-old parishioner. She says that he's not getting better and that tomorrow she will take him to the hospital," said Father Jim." "Oh, that's too bad," said Marie, "I know that this was the first time he missed Mass on Christmas." "Let's say a rosary for him," said Father Jim." So, Father Jim went to a small table in the room, and got one of his rosaries, while Marie went to the kitchen, and got one of hers. Together they said the rosary, then turned on the radio again for some more nice Christmas music, before going to bed.

In the morning Father Jim got up, and was given a nice breakfast by Marie, before Marie went out to visit with friends for the rest of the morning. There were no confessions, or other church doings, but some people still came to pay a visit to the church again to pray, as some of the Ladies of Charity led a small group of the faithful with the Stations of the Cross.

About 10:30 Father Jim drove to the hospital to see John Wane. He found out that the nurse had brought him in an hour earlier. The doctor said he could have a visitor, but just for about five minutes. So father Jim went to the room the nurse had told him that he was in, and visited with his 94-year-old friend, who was also the oldest person in town. Father Jim told him that he was praying for him, and the old man said some words in reply, but Father Jim couldn't tell what he said. So Father Jim anointed him, and left, as the doctor said he must have more rest, and that he would contact him, if he thought he would need a priest. Father Jim found out at the front desk that another parishioner, Jane Seem ore, was in now, for a lung problem, so he also visited her and gave her his blessing, before going back to the rectory to have a lunch, with some sandwiches Marie had made earlier, and left for him, with some soup to heat up, in case she didn't get back by noon.

For the rest of the day Father Jim read some passages from the Bible, as he prepared for tomorrow's homily. Marie returned a little before 5 to start fixing Father Jim's supper. Father Jim told her of his visit to the hospital. "Oh, I didn't know Jane was in the hospital," said Marie.": No, I didn't either," said Father Jim, "but I visited her. She had gone in the day before, and asked for forgiveness for missing Mass on Christmas." Father Jim said he told her that it was all right, before giving her a Christmas blessing.

The next day was December 27th, the last Sunday of 1942. The spirit of Christmas was still with everyone; the Mass was graced with the voices of 22 singers, two of their members had gone out of town for Christmas, after the Christmas Mass, and weren't back yet. They were visiting relatives on the eastern part of the peninsula and would be going to Mass at St. John's. After a somewhat shorter homily than the Christmas one, Father told the congregation of the two members who were in the hospital. "Mr. Wane is not well," said Father Jim, "I told him that we would keep him in our prayers. But the doctor said that Jane see more should be better in a day or so." The congregation nodded, they would keep their two sick members in their prayers. Some who knew John knew that John had been coming to Mass faithfully, ever since Good Shepherd was built. After breakfast Father Jim sent to the hospital again to see his 94-year-old friend John, and saw that he was about the same, and could still only see someone for a few minutes. He was still having difficulty talking, but seemed glad to know that the parishioners were praying for him.

The last thing on Father Jim's schedule was to listen to President Roosevelt's fireside chat, and then spend some time reading a short book on the saints, before going to bed.

On Monday morning Father Jim said the morning Mass, then went to the rectory for breakfast. As he was finishing he got a call from the hospital, telling him that John Wane was feeling bad. So, he went to the hospital, but, as he went to John's room the doctor said that he was stable now, that Father Jim could see him for a few minutes. Today John could speak a little, but Father Jim could see that he was obviously still having problems.

From that point on, everyone was preparing for the new year, which for the Church meant the Solemnity of Mary. A New Year's celebration was planned at the Gary Couper barn; there would be a 25 cent admission fee for the party. But this included snacks, fruit punch, and two men named Flat and Scrugs, who would be playing country, and new year's music, on a guitar, and a banjo. Cora and Andrew Zerbee would be there to celebrate something else. They had just found out that they would be having their first child in 8 months. Hans had already asked Phyllis, after the Sunday Mass, to celebrate New Year together. She said her parents would bring her to the barn, she would see him then. Father Jim also said that he would go, to give his blessing, and Marie said that she was Just staying home, she would listen to the new year come in on the radio.

Wednesday morning, after Father Jim got back from the daily Mass, he got a call from the hospital, telling him that 94-year–old John Wane was worse, upon getting to the hospital Father Jim did find John to be in bad shape, unable to talk. But the doctor said that sometimes he gets this way, then improves a little, after resting for a while. So Father Jim gave him the Last Rites. And went back to the rectory. He had supper, then prepared for some visits to some of the parishioners who might be at the New Year's party at the Couper barn.

After daily Mass on Thursday, Father Jim had breakfast, then made his rounds to some parishioners, to wish them a happy new year, and also stopped at the diner to give Phyllis Thaxter notice, that he would see her on Friday, at the party. But on Friday, after Father came back to the rectory, Marie had bad news for him. Elsie Borden called from the hospital. John Wane has just died; the time of death was 8:15 AM. "She also says she has his will, that he wrote about two weeks ago, before he went into the hospital," said Marie, "the undertaker, Joe Lando, is on his way to the hospital, to take care of things. John wrote that he wants to be buried right away, or as soon as possible, but not on Sunday. He doesn't even want a wake, unless it's a quick one," "Yes, he wasn't much for formality," said Father Jim. "At 94 years of age he didn't know many people, and his few distant nieces and nephews were a long way from here, no one even knew their addresses, or names. But he told me he had bought a plot in the cemetery, and a headstone, with just March 1848 on it, for his name and date of death. He told me he forgot which day he was born on. All that's left now for his marker is December 31, 1942." "Yes, he didn't make it to the new year," said Marie.

So, Father Jim went to the hospital, and agreed to hold a two-hour wake for John Wane, tomorrow, from 5 to 7 PM. "There will probably be just a few of us there," said Father Jim, "since it's New Year's Day. And only a few people knew him, he was the oldest person in the town, and, of course, in the parish. I'll have a funeral Mass for him Saturday, at 9 AM."

With the arrangements made for his 94-year-old friend, father Jim went back to the rectory to make his plans for Mass the next morning, and for the funeral Mass. At 9 PM Father Jim went to the Couper barn for the New Year party. Most of the people were not there yet. Gary welcomed Father Jim, and told him he didn't have to pay the 25 cent admission fee, but Father Jim told him that he insisted in putting in his quarter. "I know you aren't making any money on this," said Father Jim. "Not with all the refreshments, & after paying the two unknown men who were playing for the party, from 10 PM until the new year comes in." "Yes, they're just about to get started,' said Gary, "they settled for a total of $3 each, for 2 hours plus. If I get more than 20 people, I might just break even."

So people came in gradually, and father Jim greeted most of them, but some of them weren't parishioners, just people coming for the party. Father Jim greeted some of them also, as the two men Gary hired played mostly country, and a couple of patriotic songs, in line with the times. Only 12 people were there by 11 o'clock, but more than a dozen came between eleven and eleven thirty. Father Jim thought that with this many people, Gary might just make a couple of dollars, above expenses, which was still not much for going to the trouble for hosting a party.

Hans got there about 11:20, and greeted Phyllis, who came with her parents. As they settled in, they had some punch and snacks, and Father Jim told everyone about John Wane, and that his wake would be tomorrow at the funeral home, from 5 to 7 PM. From 10:30 on some people were dancing to good country music. But at 11: 30 their music changed to big band, and new year's music. Hans danced with Phyllis some, but he wasn't much for dancing; Phyllis did most of the leading. Then, as the clock was just shy of midnight, Hans said to Phyllis, "Wait here, I'll be right back." So Phyllis waited, and the clock struck midnight, as the two men started playing Auld Lang Syne, with all the people there joining in the song. Then Hans came up to Phyllis, with one hand behind his back. Hans then raised his hidden arm in the air, and Phyllis looked up. She saw that he was holding a sprig of mistletoe over her. She smiled, then reached up and took the sprig of mistletoe from him, and threw it behind her, and gave Hans a nice new year kiss, and a hug. "We don't need mistletoe," said Phyllis, as she gave him another new year kiss.

After the last verse of Auld Land Syne, Flat & Scrugs played one last song, show me the way to go Home, even though there was no alcohol in the punch. The people joined in with singing this song, too, as they were leaving to get home to finally go to bed, since most of them were usually in bed by 10 o'clock. Those who would be going to Mass in the morning would be allowed to receive communion, even if they had eaten something after midnight, at the party; Father Jim had given this permission, and absolution had also been given for eating meat on the Solemnity of Mary. Many people who left were still carrying noisemakers, and signs with 1943 on them.

Chapter 10

The year 1943 started with the Solemnity of Mary Mass, in memory of the Blessed Mother. Most of the choir was there, only two wouldn't be there to sing in the new year. Father Jim only briefly mentioned the war, he went on with his usual homily about Mary, and finished with telling of the wake that would be held at the funeral home for their departed John Wane, with a funeral Mass for him on Saturday morning, at 9 AM.

With the work caught up at the ranch, Hans was allowed to take Dan's truck again to go and see Father Jim, for a talk. Marie welcomed Hans in, as Father Jim told Hans to join him in the living room. "Well, is it a nice new year for you?" asked Father Jim, as they talked, near the fireplace. "It's better than I ever had," said Hans, "but I have been listening to the Blocker family saying, sometimes in relation to the war, that they're so happy to be an American, because they're free, and strong enough to go around the world to save other people from tyranny. It makes me wish I was an American, too." "Well, there are many Americans from all over the world, especially From Britain, France, Italy, Ireland, Spain, and Germany, who have become American citizens,' said Father Jim. "So, I could become an American citizen?" asked Hans. "In other times you could, but our immigration officers need to know where people are from, and it would be a problem to tell them you're from Germany, when we are at war with Germany. If you had come here two years ago, it probably wouldn't have been a problem," said father Jim. "But aren't others becoming citizens, especially when many have fled from Europe?" asked Hans. "We haven't seen many of those people here," said Father Jim, "but we do have some people coming to this part of Michigan, from Canada, each year, who become United States citizens. But they tell the border guards where they came from. You couldn't tell them that you came from Germany." "What if I tell the border men that I'm from Canada?" asked Hans. "No, the border patrols would catch you in a lie," said Father Jim, "you don't know anything about Canada, but the border agents do, they would catch you in a lie" "I'm just so worried what the good people here would think of me," said Hans, "if they found out that I'm really a German prisoner of war. And then, there's Phyllis." "Oh, I see," said Father Jim," you like her, don't you?" "Yes, I do," said Hans, "and she likes me; she kissed me at the New Year party, without a mistletoe. I've heard her say how she hares the Germans, for what they've done to the world. I think she would hate me if she knew I was German, and especially if she knew I was a prisoner of war." "Let's just think of a way to get you made an American citizen," said Father Jim, and don't think that way about Phyllis. If she loves you, nothing else will matter." "Pray for me, father, that we can find a way for me to become an American citizen. I don't want to lose all the friends I've made, either," said Hans. "We'll both pray that we can find a way," said Father Jim, "I'm glad that you came to me about this, Hans, we'll put our trust in God, He won't fail us."

So Hans went back to the ranch, and Father Jim started to prepare for John Wane's wake. He didn't expect more than a dozen or so people for it, since not many people knew the old man. But almost 20 people showed up. Most didn't know him, but were there to pay their last respects for a man who had lived about 10 years longer than most people. After visiting the casket, the people gathered around in a circle, in chairs supplied by the funeral director, as Father Jim told the people what he knew of John Wane. "His father, George, was brought up in Kansas, and met a woman from Wisconsin, and moved there, not far from the Michigan border, when he married her. John Wane was named after his grandfather, who was a well – known lawman in Kansas or Oklahoma." Then the mayor spoke up and said, "It was in Kansas, Oklahoma wasn't a state then, it was known as Indian Territory, because of the many Indian tribes brought there from the east. It may not have even become a state, but the many people who came to settle there in covered wagons changed that. They called then scooners, or maybe sooners. It wasn't until the turn of the century, around 1906, or 1907, that it was made a state. And, along with the main part of Oklahoma, they added a part of the land that had once been the most northern part of Texas." "You mean, they added a part of Texas, to the state?" asked Michael London, a rancher who was interested in history. "No." said the mayor, "the piece of land was just there, to the north of Texas. Texas had given up the land north of a certain parallel, when the Republic of Texas voted to join the union. Texas gave up that northernmost part of the Texas panhandle so it could join as a slave state. The land was just made a part of the state of Oklahoma." "That concludes our lesson in history 101," said Robert Fuller, "but what about our John Wane, father?" "I talked to him a few times," said Father Jim, "just before he finished high school a scarlet fever epidemic went through the area, his mother died from it. And shortly after he finished high school his father George came down with something, and died. John was going to get married, but on the day before the wedding his future wife was riding a horse, and the horse spooked, and threw her to the ground, where she hit her head, and died instantly. Her family and John took care of her right away. She was buried on the day she was going to get married." "That's a shame," said Victoria Gannor." "Yes, and though one or two other women there liked John," said Father Jim, "John said that he would not marry another woman, and he didn't. He lived a few miles the other side of Ottawa Creek, and went across the border into Wisconsin to go to Mass each Sunday. But he moved to Cross Bear when Good Shepherd was built, almost five years ago, as he sold his small farm and moved here, becoming the oldest person in the town, and, of course, in our parish." "Who's the oldest person in the parish now," asked

Pauline Cushman. "Irene Ryan," said Father Jim, "she's almost 87 years old." Discussions like this were not uncommon at a wake, Father Jim wasn't disturbed because his eulogy had been interrupted. It had, thought Father Jim, added to it.

So Father Jim and the others said one last prayer for John Wane, and left for home. Marie had a late supper waiting for Father Jim, and after supper Father Jim listened to the radio, while preparing his homily for the funeral Mass for this long standing member of the parish.

The next morning Father Jim was surprised to see more than thirty people in church to pay their last respects to a man only a few of them knew. Nine year old Kalex Hooper, one of the youngest of the altar boys, offered to serve for the Mass. He hadn't served for a funeral Mass before, but he saw how one of the older altar boys did it at another funeral Mass his family had gone to; he knew what to do. So Father Jim told in his homily of John Wane, for the benefit of those who were not at the wake. His casket, which was a plain pine box, as John had wished, was carried in by four men, only one of which had known John. After Mass they took the casket to the Oakridge Cemetery for burial, about fifteen people also came to join Father Jim in a final prayer for one of God's faithful, before the casket was lowered in its place.

Later that day Father Jim was visited again by Hans Kruber, who wanted to talk to Father Jim again about the possibility of becoming an American citizen. "I'll talk to our mayor about the process, without saying who it's for," said Father Jim. "Can we do it privately," asked Hans, "I don't want anyone to know I'm a German." "I don't know about that," said Father Jim, "I'll have to have a talk with the mayor, I'll keep in touch with you about it."

So, father Jim called the mayor and asked if he could get any information for someone moving to this country, who wants to become a citizen. The mayor said he would see what he could do, and call him back. Three days later Marie said to Father Jim, "Why, Robert Horton is coming up the sidewalk." "Let him in," said Father Jim, "I want to see him in my study." So, the mayor came in and said to Father Jim: "I have made a few phone calls to some places, and found out that about every month some people come over to the Upper Peninsula from Canada, to become citizens. There are two families now who have come from Canada, on the other side of St. John's, they are waiting now to meet with the government men from Lansing, to do what they need to do to become American citizens. Do you know of someone who is looking to become a citizen? "Yes, I know of someone, but what would it take to be accepted by the men from Lansing?" asked Father Jim. "I'd like to know who you are talking about," said the mayor, "I have a responsibility to the town on such legal matters." "The man is…" said Father Jim, hesitating…..."Hans Kruber." "What?' said Robert Horton, "why, he's an American, isn't he? I know he's from somewhere out of town, but he seems like any of us." "But he has a problem," said Father Jim, "he's lost just about everything but the clothes on his back on his way here. He doesn't have his birth certificate, or anything else to prove his identity. So, he wants to join in a class with others who are becoming citizens." "I see," said the mayor, "I know about the two families, all mayors and law officials are informed of this. I'll see when and where it will happen. But I know the adults have to learn about America and its history, and the laws that citizens are expected to live by. You get in touch with Hans, but he will probably have to go somewhere for about two weeks to learn what he has to, to become a citizen." "I'll get back to you on it," said Father Jim, "but keep this to yourself. In times of war, anyone who can't prove where he is from might be labeled an illegal immigrant, or even as a German or Japanese spy." "I don't think there's any danger of Hans being thought of as Japanese," said the mayor. So, as a few more days went by, the mayor told Hans what he would have to do, and that he would probably have to leave the Blocker ranch for a while to do it. Hans went to his boss, and Dan said that he understood, and that he could bring in an extra man to do Han's duties while he was gone.

Then Father Jim got a call from the mayor telling him that there would be two families from Canada applying to be citizens, one was French Canadian, they would be given their instructions in French, but they had learned some English from their 8 and 6-year – old sons, who were learning English in school. The parents were learning English in some degree from their children. The meeting for their studies would take place in some building in a town not far from Heeawatha. Father told Hans that he could go to Mass at St. John's while he was there. Clay Forester and Steven Baldwin would be representing the government, as trainers to supply the families, and Hans, with papers to study as the preliminary to taking a test for their acceptance as a United States citizen. As the kids of the parents would be naturalized with their parents. There would be more questions to be asked with Hans, since he didn't have proof of where he was born. "That will be all right with Hans," said Father Jim, "You know what a good man Hans is."

So Hans left, as Phyllis Thaxter came to the Blocker ranch to say goodbye to him. She still asked him why he wanted so much to be officially a citizen. "All of us here are citizens," said Phyllis, "we don't have to take a test for it." "I know, said Hans, "but you see, I wasn't born here in the Upper Peninsula like you were. You have a birth certificate to prove you are an American, but I don't, I don't know where mine is. I traveled across the country to get here, with no proof of identification of any kind. Don't worry, honey, I'll be back in about two weeks. I won't be in the choir for two weeks, but I understand that the town I'll be in is near St. John's, I'll go there for Mass while I'm gone." Then the Zerbee family came, to also wish him goodbye as Hans was like family to them, also. Hans then took a bus to the eastern part of the Upper Peninsula.

Hans and the two families from Canada met with the immigration officers, and were told what their schedule would be, and where they would be staying while they were there. They were given pamphlets and books about the United States, to learn as well as they could, since they would have to pass a test to make sure they knew at least most of it. Hans and the two families from Canada would have to learn of the American history, information on some of the states, some of the presidents, and the wars America had been in, up to World War I. They would also learn how the United States government is set up, and the basic laws of the land.

For 12 days the two families, with only the adults, would be studying books, and other material, with Hans. When the parents from Canada were given their own citizenship, their children would have their names put on one of the parent's paper, to make them naturalized citizens. Of course, Hans was by himself, but he was asked more questions, since he didn't come from a place in Canada to tell about, as did the two families. Hans told the truth, that he had come many miles, from the southwest somewhere, but that he didn't know where his birth certificate was. So, the officials let him continue with his studies.

After 12 days a day of rest was given for a private study by the three people, before a two hour exam was given on the 14th day. The two parents and Hans waited for almost an hour as their tests were graded, it was like high school, thought Hans, when he was waiting for the results of a final exam, to see if he would pass a course, and graduate from high school. When the officers told the people they had passed the test, they were happy, but one of the officers called Hans over to the side of the room, and told him that he had the highest mark of the five who took the test. Hans knew that this was because he was already pretty familiar with the United States, because of the training he had in north Africa, to tell him about the United States, so that he could pass himself off as an American when he would by spying for Germany. The others then wrote down the names and ages of their children on one of the parent's citizenship paper, but Hans, of course, was just given his certificate with just his name on it. Hans felt good about actually being an American citizen, without lying about himself during the questioning. "Thank you,

God,' said Hans to himself, as he took his citizenship paper and asked about when the next bus was for returning home, after first making a phone call to the Good Shepherd rectory, to tell Father Jim the good news.

While Hans was waiting for the bus, which would be there in about two hours, he borrowed a horse from the FBI, with the promise he would bring it back soon, and went to St. John's Church, to pray again to his Heavenly Father in thanks for giving him a new home, where he could continue to worship freely, as that privilege was taken away from him in his native land. He stopped to water and feed the horse, then went back to the FBI building to return the horse, and wait a few minutes for the bus. The bus that took him home got in Cross Bear a little after 8 o'clock, and Father Jim was waiting there to take him back to the rectory. Of course, he showed Father Jim his citizenship paper.

"That's great," said Father Jim, as he drove Hans back to the rectory, "did you have any problems with the government men?" "Well, one of them asked me a few times about where I came from, and even said that he might have another question for me later, but that I would be granted citizenship, partly because of the high score I got on the test. He also said that I had to report to the nearest government agency, usually the post office, and get a number for myself, so that I would be listed in that new Social Security system that the president had started a few years ago. "Could I take the car to see Phyllis," asked Hans, "I know she will be home from work now." "Yes," said Father, but I'll drive, and wait for you, to take you to the Blocker ranch.

Mrs. Thaxter answered the door, and welcomed Hans in, as she called to her daughter. "Oh, you're back!" said Phyllis, as she ran to him and gave him a kiss and a hug. "I'm a citizen now," said Hans, as he showed Phyllis his citizenship paper, with pride. Phyllis took the paper and gave it a quick glance, before setting it on a chair, and giving Hans another welcome home kiss. Phyllis' father then picked up Han's paper, and showed it to his wife, before giving it back to Phyllis. She looked at it again, then handed it back to Hans. "It's late," said Hans, "I have Father Jim waiting for me, to take me back to the ranch." As Hans walked out Phyllis gave him one more kiss, as her parents looked on, smiling. Hans answered questions from the Blockers, and settled in for the night, and called the Zerbees to let them know he was back.

Chapter 11

The word spread fast about Hans being back, and that he was a citizen. Father Jim told of him at daily Mass, and the mayor put up a sign in the town hall, saying: "Welcome Home, Hans Kruber". When Hans went to Mass again the next Sunday, the choir members all welcomed him back, with many nice words for being a citizen. Even though he hadn't been to rehearsal for the last two weeks, Hans knew the songs they were singing, and joined in with the 23 others, as usual, with some others greeting him after Mass.

The first chance he got, Hans went to the post office, with his paper of citizenship, and was given his Social Security number, which Hans thought was strange, as there seemed to be no order to the numbers. He was told that was just the way they were done, and that shortly he would have them memorized, and that he would get his official card in the mail in about a week. He was also told how the system worked, and that from now on he would be paying into the Social Security system, as all taxpayers did. So, now that he was a citizen, Hans began to look for a place to live, to have a home for himself that wasn't too expensive to buy, or rent, even if he had to continue living on the ranch, until he could make arrangements for a place of his own. He continued getting warm congratulations for becoming a citizen, and he stopped at the diner where his girl, Phyllis Thaxter, worked, as often as he could. He was always invited to have a cup of coffee, on the house, with a visit with the pretty waitress, if she wasn't too busy waiting on customers.

But more news from the war in Europe, mostly, kept coming to America. It was reported that the Allied forces would move over to begin the liberation of Europe through Italy soon, since the Allies now held all of northern Africa. This news affected Hans' girl, Phyllis, more than some people, because she still hated what Hitler had done to spread his "Master Race". One day Hans was visiting the diner, and having lunch. Phyllis found some time to talk to him about some of the news she had heard on the radio, the night before. "Oh, I just hate the Germans," said Phyllis, to Hans. "I heard more last night about reports of Germans taking the Jews, Catholics, and other people that Hitler sees as not part of his "Master Race", as he calls it. Our military isn't revealing much of the stories now, for security reasons, but I know it's a terrible thing that is happening to good, innocent people. I can't stand Germans, I wouldn't want to be in the same room with a German." "But you know", said Hans, "that many Germans came to the United States years ago, many of them have become good Americans." "I know, I'm one of them," said Phyllis. "What do you mean?" asked Hans. "My grandfather was German, he went to Ireland to marry an Irish woman," said Phyllis, "my mother is half German, with my father being an immigrant from Scotland. So, I have some German in me, but it's not the same as one who is all German." "So, your parents met in Ireland?" asked Hans. "No, they both came from Ireland and Scotland, and met in Canada, where they were married," said Phyllis, "my older brother, and sister, were born in Canada, before mom and dad moved to the Upper Peninsula, where my younger brother and I were born. My younger brother is going to get married soon, out of the Church, to the distress of the rest of us. We had all gone to Mass at St. John's, until my mother, father, and I moved here last January, in time for me to finish my schooling here." "But, I've heard, from early reports from the Pacific, of how our navy has freed some of the people on some small islands controlled by Japan, and how some American prisoners of war were freed," said Hans. "The government did not give many details of it, but they said that many American prisoners were treated very badly, with some of them locked up in solitary, and starved to death.

So, I guess we should feel the same way about the Japanese, as well." "But I still feel more of a hate for the Germans," said Phyllis. "But we need to remember, in the Bible, where Jesus tells us to love our enemies," said Hans. "Yes, I know you would remember a passage like that in these days," said Phyllis, "but I know that Jesus was more of a forgiver than we are." They finished their coffee, as Phyllis said that she would try harder to forgive everyone, even the Germans.

"I'm going to go to a private confession with Father Jim this Friday, after my work is done at the ranch," said Hans, "I didn't go to confession in the 2 weeks that I was away at Whitewater, it's been almost a month since I've been to confession." "Yes, you definitely need to go to confession," said Phyllis, "I know what an evil life you lead, Mr. Kruger." "Well, you know how bad a life I lead, better than anyone else, Miss Thaxter," said Hans, with an impish grin on his face. Phyllis then gave him a quick, playful kiss, and they didn't say anything more. They understood each other.

On Friday Hans finished his work on the ranch, then borrowed a horse to go to the rectory, for a nice fish dinner. Father Jim had caught most of the fish that day. With Father Salva's usual seconds, there was just enough for the four of them. After a short rest, Hans and Father Jim went up to Father Jim's room for a private confession. After Hans said his usual confession, which included some hate for the Germans and the Japanese, Hans told Father Jim that he was worried about his relationship with Phyllis. "Why, I thought you and Phyllis got along fine, and that you love her," said Father Jim. "Yes, I do love her, and I know she loves me," said Hans, "but we've been talking a lot, and she made no secret of the way she hates, or detests Germans, because of what they have done to so many innocent people. I'm afraid of what she will think of me, If she finds out that I'm a German. I don't want to lose her, father." "But you have a good relationship, don't you?" asked Father Jim, "are you and she close enough to consider marriage?" "Yes, I've already begun to put some money aside to eventually get a house of my own;

I'm thinking of buying that house that's on Second Street, the one that's been vacant since that older couple moved away to live with relatives," said Hans. "I know the place," said Father Jim, "the old couple left it in trust with the mayor, to get the best price he could for them. With the land that's with it, it's probably worth about $1,200, maybe $1,400 to the right buyer." "How could anyone afford that much, in these hard times," asked Hans. "Well, a person with good credit, and a steady job might get a loan from the bank, if they could get the price down to $1,000. I think the old couple might settle for that," said Father Jim. "I have money saved, but only a little over $100," said Hans, but I want to use $200 to $300 of it for a nice ring for Phyllis." "So, you want to marry her," said Father Jim, "do you know if she wants to marry you?" "Father, just as sure as the sun will rise in the morning, I know she would marry me, tomorrow, if I asked her." "I know what you mean," said Father Jim, "but take it from me, no woman I know of would want to get married tomorrow, even if you could do it that fast. I've married many couples, and the shortest time it took to prepare for a wedding was three weeks.

Most women have their wedding a month, to 5 months, from the time they're engaged. A woman's wedding day is the biggest day of her life, and she needs a lot of time for planning the place and date, where they will live, where to have their reception, whom to invite, people for the wedding party, and, of course, the bride's dress." "I understand all of that," said Hans, "but, would Phyllis even want to be with me if she knew I am German, not to mention an escaped prisoner of war?" "I know what you're saying," said Father Jim, "but if she really loves you, she'll accept you. The best thing is to stall for now, tell her you need a few months to get your life in order. It'll also give you more time to save money for making a down payment on that house, with maybe enough left for a nice ring for Phyllis. I know her, she's a nice girl, she'll be willing to wait for you." "But she's a nice girl who hates Germans, and I am one, even if I'm now a citizen," said Hans. "You just do as I said," said Father Jim, "if she really loves you, nothing else will matter."

Hans did take Father Jim's advice, and kept up with going places with Phyllis, but avoiding any serious talk about marriage. Phyllis' parents knew how much their daughter loved Hans, and were wondering why Hans hadn't yet asked her to marry him. Their younger son was married now, they went to the eastern part of the Upper Peninsula to be there for him, though they didn't like to see him get married to a Protestant woman, and go to her church, after he had spent 19 years as a Catholic. The knowledge that the woman their older son married was going to be a Catholic was comforting, but they still hated to see their younger son leave the Church.

A few days later Father Jim got a phone call from the state government, they asked to talk to Hans. Father Jim told them that he didn't live there, but that they could reach him at the Blocker ranch, and gave them the phone number. The next day Hans called Father Jim to say that the government agents called him, and that they wanted to know more about where I came from. "What do I do" asked Hans. "Did they say what they want to know, specifically?" said father Jim. "It's something to do with my name. They say it sounds German, and they aren't satisfied about the place I came from," said Hans. "Well, you do have a German sounding name, but so do many other good Americans," said Father Jim, just don't say anything about your being a prisoner of war. That's privileged information, because you were with me, in confession, when you told me." "Yes, but I still feel the need to tell Phyllis, I should not keep any secrets from her, if we're going to be man and wife," said Hans. I feel almost like I'm cheating on her with another woman, by not telling her about me." "I know how you feel, but that can wait. First, see the men from Lansing,' said Fr. Jim, "and make sure everything's all right with your status as an American. Because you're a citizen, you might, or might not be protected in time of war, when you were a prisoner of war." "But I'm a citizen, don't I have the rights of a citizen?" asked Hans, "I read about my rights in some of the books they gave me to study before I took my citizenship test." "Well, it's a fine line, in time of war," said Father Jim, "just answer the questions as if you were always a citizen, I'll be backing you up, along with the mayor, and many others who know you."

In two days the government men, "G – Men" as they were called, came to Cross Bear, and went to the mayor's office to meet with Hans, who had been notified. They met in the mayor's conference room. "Hello, I'm agent Dave Gray, FBI; that's Federal Bureau of Investigation," said the first agent, as he showed Hans his badge. The other man introduced himself as Larry Storch, as he also showed Hans his badge. "Let's get right down to it," said Agent Gray.

"We've been through your recent citizenship class studies, you do have your paper with you?" "Yes, I have it right here," said Hans, as he handed it to the men. Agent Gray looked at it, along with the other agent. "Well, it all seems to be in order," said Agent Gray, "but we still heard how you couldn't give the men running the class an exact place of origin, where you came from. You didn't come from Canada, like the two families who were in your class." "I explained to the officials how I didn't know where I was, and the fact that I don't have my birth certificate was the main reason why I wanted to have a certificate to prove that I am a U. S. citizen," said Hans. "Well, I tell you straight," said Agent Gray, "because of the war we're being extra careful of anyone who appears to be guilty of espionage, especially someone who has a German or Japanese background. But you do have rights, as a citizen, but we will still need to talk about you more, with others we answer to, in Lansing. You'll have to come with us to Lansing, to talk to our head of the Lansing office. If you weren't a U. S. citizen we would handcuff you and take you back for a week for some more questions, they will be like the ones you were asked when you took your citizenship test, but as you scored so high on your test, higher than most who were born in the U. S., we don't see that as a problem. And with your priest speaking up for you, and the mayor, we're comfortable about you, as someone who is not a spy, but for any case that possibly is involving a spy, we have to follow SOP; that's standard operating procedure. And you answered some questions that aren't usually taught by the Germans or Japanese, when they train someone to be a spy. We will make an agreement here, with your mayor, as to your visit with us being only a week. We will return you back here in a week." "I'm glad to do whatever you ask," said Hans. "Call the mayor," said Agent Gray. When the mayor came in he was told about Hans going back to Lansing for a week, but that they promised to have him back, after some more questioning. "We know that Hans will be cooperative with us," said Agent Storch, "the only way we wouldn't return him would be if we found him to be a German or Japanese spy. "Well, we sure know he's not a Japanese," said the mayor. "Oh, no," said Agent Gray, "we've already caught a few of the Japanese spies in Hawaii, and on the west coast, who look just as American as you and I look." "You mean, Americans are betraying their country." asked the mayor?" "No, since Pearl Harbor Americans have been united against the Japanese, and the Germans," said Agent Gray. "But in the last 10 or 15 years a few hundred Americans have moved to Japan, and become loyal to the emperor. The Japanese have sought these people out, and trained them for spying on us, since they still speak English, and still look like any other American. None of the spies we've caught look like they're from Japan." "I just want two things," said Hans, I want to say goodbye to my girl, she works in the diner just up the street, and I want to stop at the rectory to say goodbye to my pastor. It's on Crescent Avenue, just a little ways off the street we're on now." "All right," said Agent Gray, "but we have to leave soon, if we're going to get back to our place in Lansing tonight.'

So, the agents took Hans to the diner, only a block from the town hall. They escorted Hans into the diner, and only one customer was there, as it was early in the afternoon; he was just finishing his coffee, with a piece of apple pie. The agents just sat down near the front door as Hans saw Phyllis, who was just clearing a table. She came to see him, and he held up his hands to stop her, then said: "I'm going with two FBI agents for more questioning, to Lansing tonight." "What are you talking about?" said Phyllis." "These men have more questions about where I came from, like one of the officials did when I went to get my citizenship," said Hans, "They are satisfied that I'm not a German spy, but because of the high security of things like this because of the war, they are interrogating many people of German ancestry." "You're German?" said Phyllis, "you never said anything to me..." "I know," said Hans, "I was waiting for the right time, because I know how you felt about Germans. I'm not a spy, I'm still the same person you fell in love with." Then Phyllis turned, and went back into the kitchen. Her boss went in after her, and in about 30 seconds, walked out with Phyllis, who was obviously shaken up. Phyllis came to within a few feet from Hans, and said, "I'm all mixed up!" One of the agents then cleared his throat, and pointed to his watch, as Hans looked, and got the message. "I have to go, I'll be back in a week to be with you again," said Hans. Hans then started to walk toward the front door, until he heard Phyllis call his name. He stopped, and turned around, as Phyllis took a few steps closer to him, and stopped. She looked into his eyes, then said: "Take care of yourself," before going back into the kitchen.

As the FBI men took Hans for a quick visit to the Good Shepherd rectory, Hans said: "I've known her since August, and we've been close since September. She told me how she hates the Germans because of the things they're doing, and I agreed with her. She didn't realize that I was of German descent before, I don't know if she will ever be willing to be with me again. This is the first time, since November, that she left me, without a smile on her face, and a goodbye kiss." "We're sorry about that," said Agent Gray. If she loves you, she'll accept you."

The FBI car parked in front of the rectory, as one agent went with Hans, as he knocked on the door, then walked in to meet

Marie. "I have to talk to Father Jim," said Hans. "He's over in the church, praying," said Marie, "oh, I see him, he's coming back." Father Jim came in the door and Hans went to meet him, saying, "I have to talk to you, can we go to talk in private?" As they went into the living room Hans said how he had to go with the FBI agents for more questioning but that they assured him that he would be back in a week. "Does this have something to do with your citizenship test, or the many questions you had to answer then?" asked Father Jim. "No, it's something that could be very serious in some cases, but it's just routine with me," said Hans, "they assured me that it's just standard operating procedure. I stopped to tell Phyllis that I would be gone for a week, and she realized that I'm German." "Oh, you didn't tell her yet?" asked Father Jim. "No, I just couldn't bring myself to do it, and I think I was not right to tell her at a time like this," said Hans. "She took it hard, and I don't even know if she will want to be with me, now." "Why? what did she say?" said Father Jim. "Well, that's the problem, I just don't know," said Hans. "At first she left the room, then came back, slowly, and I told her I would be gone for a week.

Then I started to leave, but she called me, and I stopped and faced her. She came up to about two feet from me, and looked me in the eye like she's never done before, and simply said: "Take care of yourself," and walked away. I don't know what she thinks of me, father." "Well, I know how much she loves you, I think she'll accept you," said Father Jim. "That's just what we said to him in the car," said the agent, who was doing his job of listening in, as he had been trained to do in his FBI training. Father Jim gave him a cold look, and the agent went to the front room. Then Father Jim told him, in a low voice, "Just keep telling them the kind of answers that you did for your citizenship training, of not knowing exactly where you came from, and above all, don't let them know that you can speak German," said Father Jim, "it would just complicate things." "Pray for me, father,' said Hans. "I will, and I will talk to Phyllis the first chance I get, she's a good girl, and I know she loves you: I think things will be all right," said Father Jim, "you and she are too close to let something like your nationality come between you." So Hans left with the FBI men, but with doubts on what would happen at the questioning, and, above all, if his loving girl would still love him after he got back. He would do a lot of praying while he was gone.

Chapter 12

Hans and the FBI men didn't get to Lansing until almost 10 o'clock, and went right to FBI headquarters. "We have to put you in a cell," said Agent Storch, it's not so much to keep you locked up, as it is for your protection. There are a few good Americans who think it's their duty to get rid of anyone considered to be a German, or a Japanese. There are some loyal Americans who would think it's their duty to shoot someone suspected of being a spy. They would go to jail, happy with the thought that they have served their country, in their own way." "It sounds like they have forgotten the law about everyone being innocent until proven guilty," said Hans. "Yes, that's right, people forget things like that in times of war," said the agent. "You'll be treated in a decent manner, and at least one security man will go with you for meals, and to the interrogating rooms, and back to the jail for the night. We don't think you're a spy, but we still have to do these things for anyone who is thought to be German, or even speaks German," said Agent Storch. So Hans was escorted to a small cabin, much like the one he had been in when he was away for his citizenship studies.

The next morning Hans woke up on a cot, and saw something he had seen before, bars on the windows. He thought back to his days as a prisoner of war, it wasn't much different now. But a guard came and let him out, and led him to a bathroom, where could wash, and shave, and put on clothes that were almost like the prison ones he once had worn. Then two guards took him to the cafeteria. He was given a fork, spoon, but no knife to eat with. He was taken to a room, at the end of the hall of the building where the questioning would be done. A different agent, Leif Eriksson, was present, and stood behind Hans, when suddenly the agent spoke a sentence in German. Hans only paid mild attention to him, and then the agent said something else in German. Hans asked the man who he was talking to, and what it was that he said. "Sounds like German, or French," said Hans. Of course, it was a trick question to see if Hans understood German. Hans did understand what he said, but he remembered what Father Jim had said, and acted like he didn't know what the agent had said. This spared him from being asked a lot of questions about how he knew German. Then the agent waved to the door, and another agent who was watching through the window, came in for some more basic questions, similar to the ones he had been asked when he went to become a citizen, as another man wrote down everything he said.

After six days of questioning, the agents met, and talked about what they thought about this man who seemed like a good American citizen. And, because he had been so cooperative, and was spoken of highly by a priest, and a mayor, they decided that Hans must have had a lapse of the memory about where he came from, & agreed that he was not a spy, and of no danger to national security. Early the next morning the agents led Hans to a car, and gave him a ride back to Cross Bear, as they had promised. The mayor had been called about his return, so he was there to meet Hans at the town hall, along with Father Jim. Hans said the Father Jim, "I didn't make it to Mass on Sunday, they wouldn't let me go anywhere while I was being in the interrogation. Will you hear my confession?" "Well, I don't think it's really your fault, so it isn't really necessary," said Father Jim, but I'll still hear your confession at the rectory, in case you think your trip to the big city has endangered your soul."

After Hans had said his confession, he said that he had better get back to the ranch." "Dan had to get another man to replace you, since he didn't really know if you would be back. Call him and talk to him, I'm sure your job will still be there, I know you're just like family with him, too." So Hans waiter until after 7 PM, so he would be sure Dan would be in from the fields. Mrs. Blocker answered the phone. "Hello, Hans, you're back?" said the lady of the house. "Yes, I need to talk to Dan about something," said Hans. Then Dan took the phone. "Welcome back!" said Dan. "I'm ready to take up with my duties," said Hans, if you still need me,' said Hans, "I realize you hired someone else." "That won't be a problem, I can use him in a part time role, he didn't do your job very good, anyway." "I'm cleared," said Hans, "the agents brought me back, just like they said they would." "I would have your place for you, your experience is worth having an extra man on, but I have a problem, as three on my other hired hands said that they heard about you, and that they would not work with a German spy, and I can't afford to lose three men. And even if you, or I, talked to them, they wouldn't be convinced," said Dan Blocker. "So, I'm afraid I can't take you back. I'm sorry, but that's the way it is, Hans," said Dan, "if I had 3 other men to replace them, I would, you're like family." So, Hans hung up, and then asked Father Jim if he could take him to see his other "family", the Zerbees,

As Hans and Father Jim drove up to the Zerbee house Hans was greeted by Anthony and his family. "We're so glad to see you back, is everything all right now?" said Anthony. "No, said Hans, "I'm cleared as a German spy, but I can't go back to my job at the ranch because three of Dan's workers think I'm a spy, and said they would leave if I came back." "That's a shame, the way some people are these days." said Anthony, "do you know where you'll go to find a job? It's slow now for me, I don't have a place for you here. During the winter there are no crops that need tending, only some things in the barn that need fixing; let me talk with the missus, maybe we can do something." So Hans went to Andrew and Cora's house, Andrew just got back from working in the barn. "Hello, Hans,' said Cora, as she came up to him, and gave him a hug, and a kiss on the cheek. "I'm glad you're back," said Andrew, as he shook Hans' hand. "Yes, I'm not in any trouble with the government," said Hans, "and how are you doing?" asked Hans, as he looked at Cora. "I'm not showing yet," said Cora, "but in 7 months I'll be a mother." "Does Andrew take care of you?" asked Hans. "Does he!" said Cora, "he won't let me lift a finger, to move a chair, or something, He doesn't even want me to stand and wash the dishes. I tell him I'm just two months along, that I can still do anything. I can just imagine how he'll be in the last 3 months." Hans looked at Andrew, who was nodding in agreement with what his wife said.

I'm not working at the ranch anymore," said Hans, "some of Dan's workers are still looking on me as a German spy." "Why, that's crazy!" said Andrew, "I'll tell them what a good man you are." "No, they wouldn't listen to you, it would only cause more trouble," said Hans. "Your father wishes he could hire me again, but it's the off – season for farm work." "Maybe he can find something for you, I do know he needs some work done in the barn." "You're welcome to stay here," said Cora, "until you find work. Oh, how's Phyllis? I bet she was glad to have you back." "I haven't seen her yet, I have a problem with her, she walked away from me when I said goodbye to her, a week ago" said Hans. "She was upset with me." "I saw her a couple of times in town before you went away, she loves you!" said Cora. "I do think she loves me," said Hans, "but she hates Germans, and she found out that I'm from Germany." "You need to see her, and talk to her," said Cora." "Yes, but I can't do it when she's working," said Hans, "I need to go to her house at night, and see her. But now I have to go back to the rectory, as Father Jim is waiting for me. I'll be staying at the rectory tonight." "Go to Phyllis," said Cora, as she and Andrew walked with Hans back to the car.

On his way out of the farm Father Jim and Hans passed by the main house, and saw Anthony Zerbee on the side of the road, waving to them. Father Jim stopped the car, and Hans got out to see what was going on. "I've talked it over with the missus," said Anthony, "I might be able to use you, for a while, for some work on some of my machinery, but I won't be able to pay as much as I did before, when I had money from the crops."

"Anything you can give me will be fine," said Hans, "I do know some things about machinery. But now I have to go, father has to get back to the rectory." "I'll stop by tomorrow and get you," said Anthony, "you can stay here, as before."

So Hans thanked Anthony once more, and went back to the rectory with Father Jim. "That's so nice of Anthony, offering me a job, at this time of year," said Hans to Father Jim. "I'll get my things packed, for when Anthony stops to get me tomorrow." "That's good, "said Marie, "and you should go and tell Phyllis, so she'll know where you are." "I can't see Phyllis, because I have to prepare myself, because of how she feels about me," said Hans. "I'll just have to wait for the chance to talk to her at her home, where I can arrange for her to meet me." "How about meeting with her after Sunday Mass?" said Father Jim. "I'll try,' said Hans.

The next day, after going to daily Mass with Father Salva, and having breakfast at the rectory, Hans went with Anthony Zerbee, to start his new job at the Zerbee farm, again. He was given the job of fixing a harvester machine, so it would be ready for the Spring planting. In the next day Hans was assigned to do other chores, including one With Anthony, for helping to bring a load of hay to another farmer who needed it.

On Sunday Hans went to church with the Zerbee family, & sang in choir. It was just before time to sing, when Father Jim told Hans that one of the sopranos wouldn't be with the choir anymore, her husband wouldn't let her, because he was leery of Hans. "But another woman, Elsie Borden, had offered to sing before, so I got her to join. We are back to 14 women in the choir again.," said Father Jim. Even though Hans hadn't been to rehearsal because he had been letting others know he was back, he sang with the others fine, and their new soprano seemed to pick on the songs, as well. After he Mass, several people came and welcomed Hans back, they noticed that he wasn't in choir last Sunday. But Hans looked for Phyllis, and saw her about to leave the church. Hans said her name out loud, then waved to her, motioning to her to come to him. But Phyllis gave Hans a quick look, then walked out of the church. Her mother turned, and gave Hans a smile, and waved to him, before leaving with Phyllis, and her husband. So Hans knew that Phyllis' parents weren't against him, but that he would have to get to Phyllis in some other way.

Later that day Hans called the Thaxter home, from the Zerbee farm. Phyllis' mother answered the phone, and Hans said that he wanted to talk to Phyllis. Hans then heard her say: "Phyllis, come talk to Hans," In a persuasive way. Hans was glad to have her mother on his side. "Hell...., hello?" said Phyllis. "Phyllis," said Hans, "I know you're upset, I need to talk with you, and explain things." "I don't know what good that will do," said Phyllis, "you know how I feel." "Something like this can't be settled on the telephone, we need to see each other, face to face, I won't bite," said Hans. "I'll meet you at your house, or maybe on your day off.' "I guess we can do it," said Phyllis, "I have Thursday off this week, how about in the afternoon, at my house?" "That would be fine, I can get off work for it, I know Anthony will let me off work for a while, he might even let me take his truck, or at least a horse, if he's using the truck," said Hans. "I can come around 2 o'clock, and then stay around somewhere, until time for choir rehearsal, at 7 o'clock." "Bye", said Phyllis, as she handed the telephone to her mother. "Hans?" said her mother, "what's happening?" "I'm going to meet Phyllis on Thursday afternoon, at your place," said Hans, "if that's all right." "That's fine," said Mrs. Thaxter, "I'll make sure she's here. Oh, her father and I have been upset because of the way Phyllis has been, since you left for questioning." Hans said goodbye, and hung up the phone, as he felt a sense of relief, and also of dread. But at least he would be talking to the woman he loved; he would put his trust in the Lord.

So Hans worked on the farm, the Zerbee family was glad to hear that Hans was going to meet with Phyllis. On Wednesday, however, Anthony told Hans that he would be needing the truck for most of Thursday; Hans would have to take one of the good horses from the ranch, for his meeting with Phyllis. So, after lunch on Thursday, Hans hooked up Old Bessie, one of the horses Hans had ridden before, around the farm. So Hans rode the horse to the Thaxter home, where he hitched up Old Bessie. He went up to the front door and knocked on it, and was surprised when Phyllis opened the door, and motioned Hans inside. Hans saw Phyllis' mother and father sitting at the kitchen table, he smiled, and waved to them as he went by, on his way to the living room. Then Phyllis motioned to the couch, so Hans sat on it, and Phyllis sat on it, about two feet away from Hans. For about half a minute they just sat there and looked at each other, each one waiting for the other one to say something. Finally Hans said, "I sure missed you, mostly because of the way we parted when I had to go away again." "I'm still confused," said Phyllis, "I thought I loved you, but now I find out that you're a....member of that evil race." "I'm from the nation, but I'm not a man doing evil things," said Hans. "I'm sure that the bad things that are being done to Jews, Catholics, and others are only being done because Hitler, and other German leaders, are ordering the soldiers to do it. In any army, soldiers have to follow orders, whether they think it's moral, or right, or not. You wouldn't even agree to talk to me, if you didn't still love me. Forget about the German part. You told me how you are part German, but you're a wonderful woman. I love you, and I always will. Tell me that you can still love, as you did before. Our future depends on it, honey." Phyllis nodded her head a little, then looked down, at the couch. Hans then stood up. Phyllis looked up, and saw Hans motioning to her to come to him. Then she stood, and just looked at Hans for a few seconds. Then she said, "Oh Hans," and threw her arms around him. Then they just stood there, as Phyllis began to cry. "Oh, I'm so sorry," said Phyllis, as tears flowed down her cheeks. Then she looked up at Hans, and leaned forward, and gave Hans a long, warm kiss. As they parted a little, Hans took his handkerchief and wiped off her cheeks. "This is no time for crying," said Hans, "it's time for happiness, you & I are together again, and always will be, if you can put up with someone like me, for life." "I am happy," said Phyllis, as she wiped another tear from her cheek, "and I will put up with you, if you can put up with me, carrying on like this." "You just try to get rid of me," said Hans, as he kissed her again. After one more loving hug, they went out to the kitchen. Phyllis' parents beamed when they saw Hans and Phyllis walking together, with their arms around each other. "I'm only working part time now," said Hans, "but when I get steady work I'll start saving again for a down payment for that house the mayor is holding, for me and my beautiful bride." "I'm so happy that you're together again," said Phyllis' mother, as she hugged her daughter, and then hugged Hans.

Hans stayed with the Thaxter family for supper. Then, after one last kiss, and hug, Hans got on Old Bessie, and went to the church for choir rehearsal. Hans stopped at the rectory to tell Father Jim about he and Phyllis getting back together, then left for rehearsal. After, he rode the horse back to the farm, to tell the Zerbee family of his and Phyllis' reunion.

Chapter 13

Hans continued working for Anthony Zerbee, but was told that there was Not any more work to do, after he finished what he was doing in 4 days. He told Hans that he had only an occasional delivery of hay, and that he and Hans had fixed all the equipment that needed fixing. Anthony said that he was still welcome to stay there, but that he had no more work for him. He said that it would probably be easier to find another job, if he stayed somewhere in town.

So, after choir rehearsal on Thursday night, Hans asked Father Jim about him staying at the rectory, for now, until he found steady work. Of course, Father Jim welcomed him. The next morning Hans joined Father Jim for his fishing trip, since the creek wasn't frozen over. He knew that the mayor also fished where Father Jim went, so he talked to the mayor. "There's no more work for me at the Zerbee farm," said Hans, I'm staying at the rectory for now. I wonder if you know of anyone who is hiring," said Hans. "Not off hand," said the mayor, "but I do know that Dan Blocker fired one of the men he has, because he wasn't doing his work, and because he was still talking of you being a spy." "I know who it was, two others were also saying that about me, that's why I didn't go back to work at the ranch," said Hans. "They told Dan they would quit if I came back to work there." "But Dan's down a man now, do you think he might be able to have you back now?" said the mayor. "He would, but the other two men would quit, and he'd be even shorter than before," said Hans. "I might have a solution," said the mayor, I know a man, Orsen Bean, who has worked on a farm, he is looking for work, maybe he could do ranch work; and I have a man, I've been thinking of laying him off, since he's not really needed at the town hall anymore." "You mean, that if I, and these two men, came to the farm, Dan could let the two doubters go, and still have the men he needs to replace them?" said Hans. "Yes, that's just what I mean," said the mayor. "The man who works for me is Gary Bergoff. He's a pretty good clerk, but our secretary, Barbara Stanwick, can do all the secretary work. I'll let Gary know that I have to fire him, but that I have a job for him on the Blocker ranch."

So, they fished for the rest if the morning, and into the afternoon. Father Jim only caught 2 large fish, and 2 small ones, but Hans caught 3 large fish, which he gave 2 to Father Jim for their supper, and 1 to the mayor, for his help. With 4 large fish to cook, Marie had enough for supper, even with Father Salva's usual seconds.

That night Hans called the Blocker ranch, and told Dan that if he just fired the other two men who caused trouble, he would come back, with a man who had a job on a farm, and another man who could learn the job there. "I do get tired of them," said Dan Blocker, "with their constant talk about you. Let me know when you and the others can come to start, and I'll send those other two packing. They aren't very good workers, anyway." Meanwhile, the mayor called Orsen Bean at a house Orsen had left on his application, one with a telephone, and left a message for him to come to town hall for a job. He then informed his part time clerk that he had a job for him, working on a ranch. He then called Hans at the rectory, and said that he could bring the other two men up to the ranch Sunday afternoon, that they could start their new job, most likely, on Monday.

On Saturday night Dan Blocker informed his two accusers of Hans that they were fired, and could pick up their week's pay and leave by 6 o'clock tomorrow. Ty Harding and Gene Berry were surprised, one of them was even thinking of asking for a raise, for staying there. Dan didn't feel guilty about firing them, since they didn't do good work, anyway. They both complained, and said that he wouldn't be able to get others to do their work. "I already have men to replace you," said Dan, "be glad that you're getting a week's pay, you didn't earn it."

As usual. Hans sang in choir for Sunday Mass, then stayed at the rectory until mid afternoon, when Father Jim took Hans to the Blocker ranch. Soon afterward the mayor brought Orsen Bean and his former employee, Gary Burghoff to the ranch, & left. Father Jim said to Dan, "Do you think these men will work out for you?" "Yes," said Dan, "I'll have the man who used to work on a farm work with one of my other men, and the former town employee can work with Hans, he'll show him the ropes about working on a ranch. I'm glad to get Hans back, not only do I get a good day's work from him, but he's a good friend, as well." "But it won't be a problem for Hans to get to choir rehearsal on Thursday night?" asked Father Jim. "No," said Dan, "he can take the truck, I don't use it that late in the day."

So Hans was back to work again, and showed Gary how they got things done on a ranch, and the other man was also working out fine. Hans took every chance to visit the diner where Phyllis worked, and assure her that he was saving whatever he could out of his pay, for what he would need for a down payment for the house that they both wanted. One day when Hans was having a nice talk with his intended, his girl said; "I've been saving what I can, maybe, with what we both have, we could get the house sooner." "How much do you have saved?" asked Hans. "I have more than sixty dollars," said Phyllis, "I've been saving since I started working, hopefully for my wedding, if I met the right guy," said Phyllis. "So, do you think you'll ever meet your prince charming?" asked Hans. Phyllis put her forehead to his, and smiled. Hans didn't need an answer. I used to have more than $40, but when I went away for questioning I had no income, and only got one or two dollars a day when I was working for a week, at the Zerbee farm. I was down to $18, but now I'll start to save again. I already have almost $40, but

I know that I'll need $150, maybe $200 for a down payment, if the owners are willing sell it through the bank, and get paid then." "The house will be for both of us," said Phyllis, "let me give you what I have, after I get paid on Saturday, I should be able to give you at least $50. With your money we should have about $100. You can tell the mayor to contact the people who own it, that we will pay $1,000 for the house. By the time we make arrangements with the bank we should have $150 to use for a down payment, and finance the rest."

"Yes, and we can start making plans for..." said Hans, but a kiss stopped him in mid – sentence.

Thursday night Hans stopped at the rectory to talk to Father Jim about his and Phyllis' plans for the house. "We'll also start making plans for our wedding." "Have you thought of who you will want to marry you two?" joked Father Jim. "Why, father," said Hans, "you know we wouldn't want anyone but you." "I'll be happy to do the job," said Father Jim, "you two are a perfect couple." "Well, if she can put up with me for a lifetime, she'll be a saint," said Hans. "I think you will both learn to put up with each other, said Father Jim. Love will overcome any differences you may have."

So, Hans went to choir rehearsal, and then back to the ranch, in Dan's truck. While Hans was at rehearsal Father Jim got a phone call, and after a few minutes, hung up the phone. "What was that about?" asked Marie. "Bad news," said Father Jim, "do you remember how Ruth Owen told us a couple of weeks ago about how pleased she was to get a letter from her son Buck, who had fought in north Africa, and was fine? Some words on his letter were blackened out, for security reasons, but she could make It out that he was on a ship in the Mediterranean, south of Italy." "Yes, wasn't it in the news that we would be sending our forces to invade Italy sometime?" said Marie. "Yes, but Ruth just told me that her son was on a frigate, and that a German U Boat sunk it. She said that Buck was burned in the explosion, and went down with the ship, along with seven others who were drowned, though they were able to recover six of the bodies, but Buck was one of six who was drowned. One of the Americans tried to hold on to him, and did, but he was drowned. After a search of the area, the navy declared the other men who went down with the ship as lost in action. One who got a glance at his burned body said that it was better for him to go the way he did, he would have had a miserable life, if he had lived. The flag covered coffin just got here this morning, they sent two officers to come here and see that his burned body was given a decent, military funeral. I'll hold a wake for him tomorrow afternoon, with his burial afterward. It will be a closed casket, of course, because of his extensive burns."

The two army men stayed in the hotel overnight, while Father Jim arranged for the casket to be moved to the church. After Mass was celebrated, by Father Salva, Father Jim prepared, for the funeral. He did his job to visit the family, as was his duty in the family's time of grief. Ruth Owen's husband had just returned from a trip out of town, and found out what had happened. The family needed Father Jim's support, as the young man also had a younger brother and sister, aged 16 and 13, to mourn him.

The two army men, Lieutenant Rivers, and Sergeant Connor, had eaten their breakfast where Phyllis worked. They just ordered eggs and toast, and coffee, for a breakfast, and ordered a beef dinner for lunch; they weren't Catholics. The diner always offers a fish dinner as the daily special on Friday, which all the Catholics have. Then the flag covered casket was moved to its proper place in the church. Father Jim sent word to the family, and some others that the viewing of the closed casket would be from 2 to 3 PM, with Mass following. The casket was placed in the center aisle, at the front of the church, with the Owen family seated at the front pew, to greet friends and family members who came to pay their last respects, as they told the family how sorry they were for their loss of a son, and brother. Then, at 3 o'clock, with many of the people still in the church, Father Jim went to the podium to give his eulogy.

"My good people," said Father Jim, "we are here to say our farewell to Buck Owen, a cherished member of this church, and of the community. After graduating from high school last June, Buck joined, with several other men from our area, our military forces, to serve their country. We did, of course, hope that all these brave young men would return to us after the war was over, but we also knew that it was only a matter of time before we would mourn our first victim of the war. Buck Owen is the first to come back to us, as a man we are all proud of, for doing his part in the defense of our freedom. He died a horrible death, but it came quickly, by drowning, along with others who were also lost, with the ship that he was on. He had served in the battle for north Africa, and was on his way to fight again somewhere else, but he never got a chance. He was in the reserve columns in the battle for north Africa, and never took a human life. He was a faithful member of Good Shepherd, and we all now offer our condolences to his mother and father, Ruth and Jack Owen, and to his close sister Cynthia, and brother Jacob. If any family member wishes to say something, they may come forward. If not, we will proceed to the cemetery, where Lieutenant Rivers and Sergeant Connor will conduct a military service, after I say my prayers for Buck.

So, the coffin was again taken to the military vehicle, and the army men then followed Father Jim to the cemetery. Six volunteers acted as pallbearers, to bring the casket next to the grave that had been dug earlier by the cemetery employees. After Father Jim gave his final prayers of commitment, the two army men took the flag that covered the casket, and folded it up in a usual military way. Then the lieutenant took the folded up flag, and walked to Mrs. Owen, and bent over slightly, holding out the flag. Ruth hesitated, then reached forward, and took the flag. The lieutenant gave her a salute, then went back to where the sergeant was standing, and they both went back to the army vehicle, and started back to the army base in the southern part of Michigan. Then the cemetery people took hold of the ropes under the coffin, and carefully lowered the casket into the grave. Then they started shoveling the new pile of dirt into the grave, as Father Jim, and the family, looked on for a few minutes, then left for their homes. They had arranged for a headstone to be carved, and placed on the grave, in a few days. Earlier, the mayor told Ruth and Jack that a red heart would be placed next to Buck Owen's name on the list of men who had gone to war, to show that Buck Owen was gone, nut would still be loved, and remembered.

On Saturday several people who weren't at the church, or the cemetery, came by the Owen house to give their condolences. Father Jim mentioned Buck in his homily on Sunday, as a few more tears were shed by the Owen family members.

Chapter 14

With their first casualty of the war, the parish, and the community became more aware of what was going on overseas, especially when plans were being made for the eventual liberation of Europe, eventually from Africa, and from England. Also, recent reports told of how the U. S. Navy was beginning to progress with its "island hopping" campaign in the Pacific. It was reported that these defeats began last year, when, for the first time in 50 years, the Japanese Navy suffered its first defeat when it tried to take a small atoll, called Midway Island, to use as a jumping off point for a bombing of Hawaii. Although the United States lost an aircraft carrier, and some men and planes, in the end, Japan retreated back home. Four of Japan's finest aircraft carriers had been sunk by planes from three American carriers, along with many of Japan's planes. But, more importantly, more than a thousand of Japan's veteran pilots, and others, were lost, which Japan would have a hard time replacing. It was a hard blow for the Japanese to take; they suddenly realized that they were facing a strong opponent, more than they had in their years of conquest in China, and most of southeast Asia. But they still revered their emperor, and were confident that they could hold on to the lands they had conquered.

Meanwhile, many members of Good Shepherd Church were going around to people's houses, for donations for helping the Owen family pay for their funeral, and headstone expenses. They were one of the needy families, and had been given $20 after the August fundraiser, but it just helped pay for bills they had then.

They had no money set aside for the unexpected death of their son, Buck. A headstone would cost $18, half of which was for the engraving, which included Buck Owen's name, his date of birth, date of death, and the words KILLED IN ACTION. Although Hans and Phyllis were saving what they could for a down payment on the house, they gave $10 for the Owen family's cemetery and headstone expenses. The total cemetery expense of $62 was reached, with just the $18 left for the stone. But the two men who chiseled on the stone said that they would settle for $12, so the mayor took $5 out of petty cash for a town need, as he and two other town employees each put in $2, & a visitor put in the last dollar, so that everything was paid for the Owen family.

The mayor then told Father Jim, and others that when the FBI men were done with questioning Hans they would keep him up to date on some things that were going on with the war, things that weren't top secret that would endanger national security. "I'm going to hold a meeting for the community on the latest war news, on some items that might not be reported in the papers, or over the radio," said Robert Horton. I'll be writing everything down, and on Friday, at 7 PM, I'll have a gathering I the town hall to keep us all up to date, as much as possible." So, the word was passed to the church members, and others, with a sign put up in the town hall announcing the mayor's own meeting about the war. The meeting room in the town hall was filled with extra chairs as more than 30 people showed up for the meeting, with some having to stand. Then the mayor came in and said: "I've invited all of you here to become more informed on how the war is going, as much as we know about that isn't top secret, as much as is possible. The news came out months ago about our armies taking north Africa back from the Germans. With a partial control of the Mediterranean Sea, including the important Suez Canal, it is expected that we will use our position to eventually take action against the southern part of Italy, to take that part of Europe, until the rest of the

German – controlled territory can be freed. It could be going on right now, but we won't get any details, until we have at least gained control over the southern portion of Italy. Does anyone here have a question?"

Shawn Tovey spoke up and said: "How are our forces doing in other parts of Europe? I've heard some news about the Germans in Russia, but not many details yet." "I've received information on that," said the mayor, "we all heard of when Germany invaded Russia in 1941, and caught Russia off guard, since they had a nonaggression pact with Germany. Russians had come in and taken part of Poland when Germany invaded this peaceful country, so it looked like they were allies here. But it was still a gathering of the spoils of war, for Germany and Russia were traditional enemies. So Germany used their powerful Luftwaffe, the German air force, to push their way into Russia, with the object of taking Moscow, and forcing Russia to surrender. But they had so much land to cover that the German forces were spread thin, and then the harsh Russian winter made it hard on the German armies. The Germans were within shooting range of Moscow, but couldn't get any farther, since some of their forces were sent to the east, to the city of Stalingrad, an important industrial city. But the Russians brought in thousands of men from the east, to defend Stalingrad. Though the Luftwaffe bombed the city into rubble, the Russians held on to the main part of the city, with the help of American planes dropping off food, medicine, and ammunition to help hold off the Germans. Then, eventually, the Russians were able to send in forces from the south, and the north, until they were able to completely surround the mighty German 6th Army. Germany tried to fly supplies in to their army, but the Russians had good anti-aircraft guns set up, so that on no day did Germany get enough supplies through to the army. The general in charge finally had to surrender the whole 6th Army to the Russians, who, after taking into their confinement the higher German officers, shot many of the remaining Germans so that they wouldn't have to keep them, and feed them as prisoners of war. The Russians were holding on elsewhere. Despite the shelling and bombing the Germans did, Moscow still stood, and Leningrad, which the Germans had surrounded for two years, still clung desperately to life. Germany moved some troops away from Moscow and Leningrad to fight against the advancing Russian troops. Germany moved some troops up from Italy to help in the fight, making Italy more vulnerable to Allied forces from the south. But Germany was fighting a losing battle with the Russians. This is, no doubt, bringing the day closer for our forces coming across the English Channel, to liberate France, and the rest of the German held territory. But it was slow going with the Russians, even if they were advancing. A piece if information was passed along from an American reporter, who came in a supply plane. It was just before Christmas, and Russian and German troops were lined up in trenches, about 15 feet apart, like it was in World War I. The reporter was behind the Russian lines, as both sides were firing back and forth. Then a Russian produced a hand victorola from somewhere. The Russians put a record on, with classical music, and the shooting stopped on both sides, as both Russians and Germans loved classical music. Then the record finished, and as a Russian took the record off to put another one on, a German who could speak Russian stood up and called over to the Russians, saying, in Russian: "Play more Bach; we won't shoot." So, it looks like there are some humane moments, even in time of war. But the real challenge will be to get past the Germans entrenched along the French border of the English Channel. The Germans will have to be made weaker to some degree, and be caught by surprise before our forces can begin the liberation of Europe. Does that answer your question?" said the mayor. Everyone nodded, and said that they had learned a lot of things they didn't know before. "We will have another meeting next Friday, but I might not have much more to report, other than the latest in the battle for the North Atlantic. But word could come anytime about the invasion of southern Italy," said the mayor.

So, the people left, with a new outlook on the war, especially about the German defeat at Stalingrad, and in other parts of Russia. They would pass this information to others, and the mayor asked Father Jim if he could borrow about 15 or 20 chairs from the church, since he knew that there would be even more people there for the next meeting.

Meanwhile, Hans and Phyllis had put together, with their last paychecks, $150 for a down payment for the bank loan for the house. The woman who used to live there agreed to take $1,000 for the house, and property, at the end of 2ndStreet. Father Jim went with Hans and Phyllis to Cross Bear Bank, to cosign for the loan, since Hans didn't have any property to put up for the loan. The bank figured out a 36 month mortgage plan, Hans would have to pay $24.75 for the remaining $850 on the loan, after the bank received $150 down payment. They would be able to pay the $24.75 to the bank, and still have money left for furnishings, and other things for the house, so it would be ready for them when they were married. Hans also opened up another savings account to put in money for the wedding, but it would be mostly for buying Phyllis' wedding ring. It was February when the loan was signed by Hans, with Father Jim signing as the cosigner. The first payment would be due March 10th, and on the 10th of each month afterwards. Hans and Phyllis already had $12 on hand toward the first monthly payment, but they, as a team, would have to work at getting the house ready to live in.

Phyllis was already planning for the garden she would have, near the house, where the older woman used to have one. Hans and Phyllis started talking about their future, the day after the signing of the loan.

"It'll be a little while longer before we can get married," said Phyllis, if we got married now the house wouldn't be ready for us, we need time to save money to get the things we need." "Yes". said Hans, "and I'm going to try to get you a better ring than the ones we looked at." "Any ring will be just fine," said Phyllis, "I don't care if only one third to one half of a carat, as long as it's from my loved one." Those are the $80 to $100 ones I was thinking of," said Hans, "we're saving for the wedding, but I want to use most of my savings for a larger ring, as you'll be wearing it for the rest of your life." "But we're both setting money aside for our wedding, so it's my money, too," said Phyllis," I have a say for how much is spent for a wedding ring?" "No, what we're saving now is just for that our wedding," said Hans. "And ever since we became engaged I've been saving money just for the ring, every dollar or dime I can get; I don't need anything else but you. "Ever since we were saving for the down payment on the house I've been doing some extra jobs at the ranch, and in some other places. I already have more than $50 saved to get you the ring you deserve." Then Phyllis gave Hans a nice kiss and hug, and told him how much she loved him, for all the work and sacrifices he was doing for her. "Hey, you're working hard, too" said Hans, "and the sacrifices that I make aren't just for you, they're for us. We can't get married as soon as we would like, we may have to wait three, maybe four months before we'll be ready to start life together. But it will be worth it, we'll have stories to tell our children someday." "And our grandchildren," said Phyllis. "That brings to mind Cora Zerbee," said Hans, "we thought we would be married long before their baby comes, but with her due date in late August, we might be married just a few weeks before the birth. And they have asked us to be their Godfather and Godmother." "I know," said Phyllis, "but when he or she grows up they will know that Mr. and Mrs. Kruger are their Godparents. Oh, I forgot to tell you, Penny Marshal, who works in the dress shop not far from the diner, used to step in for lunch two or three times a week, but she has been out of town for more than a month, looking after some sick relatives in Wisconsin. She just returned a few days ago, and said to me, "well, how's married life, Mrs. Kruger?" Of course, I had to tell her that we had postponed our wedding until about June. She thought that we would be married soon. I told her that she could still call me Mrs. Kruger, if she wished, that I would answer to it." "Do you think you can get used to being Mrs. Hans Kruger?" said Hans. "Oh yes, I'm going to love being Mrs. Hans Kruger," said Phyllis. "Father Jim has been wondering just how long it will be before he marries us," said Hans, "you have this Thursday off, I can get Dan to let me come to town for supplies, and we can stop and see Father Jim, and explain how we will have to wait until mid, maybe late June."

So, on Thursday, Hans took Dan's truck, and got some groceries, & some items needed for branding. At one P. M. he stopped at the Thaxter house to pick up Phyllis. He drove to the rectory to meet with Father Jim. "So you see," said Hans, we have so many things to save money for to get the house ready for us to move in when we're married, besides making that monthly payment to the bank, we won't be ready to get married in three weeks, as we originally thought." "You'll still be there to marry us in June, won't you, father?" asked Phyllis. "Yes, you two just get done whatever you have to, just decide on a date and let me know," said Father Jim. Then Father Jim said, "You know that first meeting with the mayor about the war was really an occasion with the community. I've had a few people tell me what Robert said, especially how the situation is with the Russians and the Germans fighting. We've never had a community get – together like this about a national event, but, then again, we've never had a war like this before, where most of the countries in the world are on one side or the other. A number of countries, like Switzerland and Sweden, are neutral, but even some of the neutral countries are trying to help with refugees, mostly from the German occupied nations, and with many of the Chinese who have been driven back from their homes and cities, by the Japanese. World War I was supposed to be the war to end all wars, but, as we can see, it certainly was not. Britain and France should have stopped Germany when it began to take over other lands, without a shot being fired, but they didn't want to do anything that might cause war. It took the invasion of Poland for France and Britain to realize that they had to stand up and fight Hitler. The United States also didn't want war again, and stayed officially as a neutral country, until Pearl Harbor brought us into the war." "We heard about it, also," said

Hans. "Phyllis has to work until about 8 o'clock, with the closing of the diner, but Dan Blocker says he's going to go to the one tomorrow night, and his son and I will go with him. A few of the women don't want to go, because they don't want to hear anything about the war. Cora will be staying at the main house with Andrew's mother, they'll be talking about other things, like about when Cora's baby is born, I guess. A meeting like that can always help, especially when a woman is expecting her first child. The mother–in–law, or her own mother, can be a big help for a soon to be new mother. But I know Andrew, and Cora, pretty well, and I think Cora will be a fine mother. And, from the way Andrew has been waiting on Cora all the time, I think Andrew will be a good father, too." "Just think," said Hans, to Phyllis, in time we'll be going through the same talks and worries that a first–time mother usually has." "Let's just concentrate on getting married, first," said Phyllis.

Chapter 15

Word had gotten around about the first meeting the mayor had held, so on this Friday almost 60 people showed up for this week's talk. There were not enough chairs for everyone, even with extra chairs from the town hall, and with the 15 or 20 chairs borrowed from Good Shepherd Church, ones that were used for Mass on Christmas and Easter, when there was always standing room only. Some people were standing in the hall leading into the room, many others were standing by the walls, next to the chairs that had been put in place by the mayor and some helpers. For the last week many people had been listening to the news about the war on the radio, so the mayor would have an informed audience.

"Hello everyone," said the mayor, as he started the meeting, "I'm sorry we don't have enough space for all of you to be seated, this meeting room was built for smaller groups, like 15 or 20. It would be nice if we had a larger place to meet." "How about a church?" said Steve Raines, one of the Good Shepherd parishioners who were present. "Well, we would have to check with Father O'Connell about that," said the mayor. The church has its own schedule for prayer meetings, and other things, we wouldn't want to impose on whatever the church has going on, as it's always open for prayer visits from anyone, as well. Also, many people who are here tonight aren't parishioners, and might not know where Good Shepherd is. Of course, we could put up a sign with directions to the church. But in the meantime, if we do meet here again next week, I'm asking some of you to stay home, and only bring one or two members of each family, so that we won't have to turn away some people, because we don't have the room for them. Steve, will you talk to Father Jim about this?" Steve Raines nodded, that he would see Father Jim about it.

"Now," said the mayor, "I don't have as much to talk about as I did last week, but first I would like to hear from any parents who have heard from their son who is in the military, if you wish." A few people raised their hand, as in a school classroom. "I see Pearl Hart, right near the front," said the mayor, "what would you like to say?" Pearl stood up and said, "I got a letter from my James, he said that he was fine, that he and others who were in his group were finished with their basic training, and that they would be going on a ship to – and then the next word or words were blackened out by the military." "Yes," said the mayor, "that's always done with letters sent to home, for security reasons. They want to make sure that no information gets through to a German or Japanese spy, to tip them off as to where we're going and what we are doing. I heard that the letters we send are also checked, before being given to the soldier. It's all in the name of national security. I see another hand, all right, Mrs. Murphy." Mrs. Murphy stood up and said, "My son Audie sent me a letter saying how there was an explosion this week of some kind in the kitchen of the ship he was on, and he and another man were injured, but that his left arm was just scratched from his fall, and after a day in sick bay he was back on the job. Then he said they were all headed for-, and then that part was blackened out, as with Mrs. Hart's letter." "That's fine," said the mayor, "it looks like Audie Murphy will be all right, and make a good showing of himself, even if he did, as you told me, Mrs. Murphy, have, at first, some reservations about going to war, because of his Christian upbringing."

The mayor then cleared his throat, and said, "I guess our young men are doing all right, there have been a few reports of some casualties of British and Americans who were just found in northern Africa, in the desert, with a few Germans who right away surrendered when they saw that they were alone. I've heard from the FBI this week. There's not much change in the fighting in Russia, but Russia is slowly retaking the land that Germany has held since they invaded Russia in 1941. They estimate that millions of Russians, including many civilians have died since the invasion, more than any other nation, including Germany. But there was a report from the British and the American navies, saying that they sunk two German U – Boats, but they couldn't find any evidence from the breakup of the ship. They said that they probably just sunk to the bottom, without blowing up. None of our ships or submarines were lost. That's about it, except that although London is still being bombed by Germany, but not as much as it was before. American and British ships stationed along the British coast, and more antiaircraft fire have shot down a lot of planes, either over England, or in the English Channel. The addition of American forces has bolstered Britain's resolve and guaranteed that there will be no invasion of England, as our intelligence agents had reported, that Hitler was planning to do. And, in my own opinion, I think Hitler would have done, if he didn't have his hands full of the war with the Russians. The staunch people of London have succeeded in holding off the Nazi attack, and the whole free world admires them for their dedication, & for the sacrifices they have made for their families, and their country. Well, that's about all for now, we'll see you next Friday, but if we meet here again, remember what I said about just bringing one or two from each family, unless we can meet in Good Shepherd Church. And I thank Mrs. Hart and Mrs. Murphy for their report on their sons. We hope the letters we get will all be good news, even if we won't know where our brave young will be, as they carry out their work for God and country." Many people applauded for the good report from the mayor, and said they would be there again.

Father Jim wasn't at the meeting, but got word the next day from the mayor about the suggestion made to have the meeting in the church, because of the many people who had to stand, despite the extra chairs that were brought in. Father Jim didn't hesitate, he told him that he would gladly open the church for a meeting. The chairs he had loaned for the last meeting could be brought back to the church, but probably wouldn't be needed, since the church was built to seat more than 250. "That's fine," said the mayor, "I'll put up a notice in the town hall, and have some others put up to let people know, and for giving directions to Good Shepherd for the ones who are not parishioners." "That's fine," said Father Jim, all are welcome in our church, and who knows, we might even convert a few." "But that's not what you're going to do, really," said the mayor. "Of course not," said Father Jim, "I was just, you know, kidding. But we also wouldn't turn anyone away, should they want to join our church." "I'll be bringing back the chairs I borrowed, so you can have them on hand for the two times a year when you need them, you know when I mean," said the mayor, as Father Jim chuckled in agreement. Father Jim knew which days he meant.

Many people who were at the last meeting saw the notices that were put up in different places of businesses, at the post office, and, of course, at the diner where many people went to during the week. An added note was on the notice to bring the family, if you wish, since there would be enough seats for everyone. It also told where Good Shepherd Church was, and how to get there. "If I put up a note that we will be closing at 6:30 on Friday," said Phyllis' boss, to Phyllis, "we can make it there, also, what do you think?" "That sounds fine, I hope I can find the church," said Phyllis, as she looked away. "Oh, you know where it is," said her boss, with a grin on her face.

Meanwhile, life went on at the church, and for Hans and Phyllis, as they went on with their work, and put some money aside for the monthly payment on the loan, and for furniture, and for other things they would need for the house. Hans was also doing some extra work for Dan Blocker, things that weren't included in the regular job he had on the ranch. This helped Dan, also, since he didn't have to hire someone else to make a delivery, or something else that an outsider might not know how to do in a proper manner. Hans kept putting this extra money in his account for the ring he was going to get for Phyllis, he now had almost $65, enough for buying one of the cheaper rings they had looked at, but he was being driven, inwardly, toward getting the larger ring Phyllis had only glanced at. Hans and Phyllis met for about an hour or so, on her day off, unless he had a job to do on the ranch, or somewhere else. But they always met for a half hour or so after Mass on Sunday. On this Sunday they met for a few minutes with Andrew and Cora, near the entrance of the church. "You look tired," said Phyllis, to Hans. "Yes, I've had a busy week at the ranch, and with an extra job I did on Wednesday. But I think I'll go to the store where I worked, the owner said he had some work to take care of, I'm sure he would give me something for helping him," said Hans. "You're already tired," said Phyllis, "you go and have breakfast, then go to the ranch & rest for the rest of the day, you hear me?" "All right," said Hans. Then he said to Cora and Andrew: "How do you like that? We're not even married yet, and already she's telling me what to do." Cora and Andrew just smiled.

Phyllis wasn't the only one who noticed how hard Hans was working. "Father, I'm getting worried about Hans," said Marie, at breakfast. "He's working all the time, except for when he sees Phyllis, a couple of times a week, I'm afraid he'll burn himself out." "He'll be all right," said Father Jim, "he's a strong young man. It's the same with the rest of the nation during these times, everyone is working hard to pay the bills, and to help with the war effort." "Yes, the war," said Marie, I guess we should think more of our young men who are on their way to, or already are in battle, like our men fighting against the Japanese, in the Pacific. I hate war, but there's nothing that will be more honorable than putting one's life on the line for God, and country. This is the month of February, shouldn't we be planning for our instructions for our six to eight year olds for their instructions for their first Communion?" "We still have time," said Father Jim, "Ash Wednesday doesn't come 'til March 10th, we only need 4 or 5 weeks to get them ready to receive the Blessed Sacrament for the first time, on Easter. And Easter isn't until April 25th,

I think, we have plenty of time." "Easter comes late this year, then," said Marie. "Yes, we still have a couple of weeks before we start checking our records for the children, usually aged 7 or 8, to get them ready for instructions, in the weeks of Lent," said Father Jim. Last year two of our families held back their 8 year olds, they didn't think they were ready for understanding the true meaning of the Holy Eucharist." "So, they will be 9 now," said Marie, "We'll have to convince their parents that they are old enough now." "I think I saw them in Mass a couple of times, looking on as their friends that were their same age, going up to receive, and knowing that they still couldn't, yet," said Father Jim. "Maybe the Church could set a rule for this," said Marie. "No," said Father Jim, "the Church has enough rules, something like this has to be left up to the parents, to decide when their children are ready."

In the town, word got around about the mayor's next meeting. Several people called the rectory asking for directions to Good Shepherd Church. And though a few of the people left their children at home, because of what the mayor had said about the cramped spaces in the town meeting room, many Good Shepherd parishioners told others to bring the family, they knew there would be enough room for them in their church, since they knew the church would hold more than 250 people, without any need for extra chairs. Some friendships were made, also, when some people who lived on the outskirts of town, and didn't have a car, were given a ride to the meeting, by a nearby member of Good Shepherd.

On Friday night more than the 58 people who were at the previous meeting were there in Good Shepherd Church, with others, as more than 90 people came. The people in town were getting more interested in news from the war, especially since 17 area families had sons overseas, except for the Owen family, whose son had been returned to them as Cross Bear's first casualty of the war. A few people came in after the mayor started the meeting, as they had a hard time finding the church, but there was plenty of room for them.

At 7 o'clock the mayor stood in the middle of the church, near the altar, and motioned for silence to the crowd. Everyone settled down, and the visitors stopped looking at the statues, stained glass windows, and other things that you couldn't see from the outside of the church. Father Jim and Father Salva were sitting in chairs near the altar, and the mayor introduced them, for the sake of the visitors who didn't know them. Then the mayor went to the podium.

"First of all," said the mayor, "I want to thank Father O'Connell for giving us his church for our meeting. Those of us who were with us last week know how it was crowded, even with extra chairs brought in, as our town meeting room wasn't built to hold 60 people. I would guess there are at least 100 people here tonight, or close to it. Many of you are here for the first time. The reason I'm giving you up to date information on the war is because the FBI, when they were here in Cross Bear recently, agreed to pass on to me things that weren't top secret, but also things you might not hear on the radio. I'll give you the bad news first. Last week I told you of the possibility of our navy sinking two German U-Boats. But two days ago one of our American destroyers was sunk by a U-Boat, in the north Atlantic. They reported that 17 men died in the explosion, as the rest of the men abandoned the sinking ship in life rafts, except for 8 men who were taken down, as the ship sunk. Two of them were recovered by divers, and their bodies will be sent home for burial, as men who died in the service of their country. The other six weren't recovered, he was known as the son of the McRae family, Joe McRae. He will be listed as missing in action, for now, but the FBI said that a thorough search was made of the area, and they will officially listed as lost at sea. The McRae family, which lives a few miles out of town. Will not be able to give their son a burial, as we did with the Owen man, a few weeks ago. But the FBI told me that a year ago the German U-boats ruled the north Atlantic, and many cargo ships from the United States or Canada were often not reaching England. But since then more than 30 U-Boats have been confirmed sunk, and many others trying to get back to the French coast for more supplies, and torpedoes. We are now winning the battle for the north Atlantic. And there is much talk about our forces in north Africa invading southern Italy soon, to begin the liberation of Europe. And, in the last 6 months the buildup of men and war machines in Britain have guaranteed that England is safe from a German invasion. There is very little bombing of London and other places in England now, as the American and British planes have shot down many of the German planes. Military experts say that Germany's air power is only 40 % of what it was a year ago, because of the many planes shot down over England, or over the English Channel. Germany has also less planes because they have had to send some to fight against the Russians. Most Germans have pulled away from the encirclement of Leningrad, which had been so, since the beginning of Germany's attack on Russia, in 1941. Now we are able to bring food and other supplies to the people there, who probably wouldn't have been able to hold the Germans off much longer. In the future we will likely hear of our men being injured, killed, or taken as prisoners of war. But we can pray for all of our fighting men, including the ones from Britain, Canada, France, Australia, New Zealand, and India. Now, Father O'Connell has something to say, I saw him wave to me." Father Jim walked over to the podium and said; "I'm so glad to see so many of you here tonight, the mayor will hold a war meeting here every Friday. We should be prepared for some bad news from time to time, but it's always darkest before the dawn. And I'm holding a special prayer get-together here, tomorrow morning, for all of our men overseas, starting at 10 AM. Father Salva," said Father Jim, motioning to him, "will be hearing confessions for an hour, until 10 o'clock. I'll hold the service, with readings from the Bible about war, and a couple of specially selected hymns, sung by the members of our choir who are here. After about a half hour I'll lead with the rosary, with our Ladies of Charity, for the safety of all our troops. We also welcome our non – Catholic friends to join us for this, if you wish. Our members will show you how we say it, we will give you a rosary. I hope many of you can join us, God hears all of our prayers, it doesn't matter which church we belong to. You can also just sit with us, and listen as we pray.

So the people left, and Father Jim knew one of the people who lived near the McRae farm, so he asked them to stop by and make sure they knew about their son, Joe, who was officially lost in action, and the 2nd casualty from the Cross Bear area. "It's better to hear it from one of us, in case they haven't been notified yet. Who Knows, they might even want to come to our prayer service," said Father Jim. Phyllis Thaxter kept on with saving as much as she could toward her and Hans' wedding, with a little set aside for home furnishings, and Hans put aside as much as he could, for the same things. Hans also kept up with doing odd jobs when he could, as he came in town when he could be spared from the ranch to work in the store he once worked in, or for chopping wood, or for making some deliveries for some businesses with people out of town who didn't have a car or truck. He also stopped to pay a quick visit, when he could, at the rectory, or the church, where he said a rosary, and sometimes lit a votive candle. One day he stopped and talked to Father Jim about how much money he had saved for Phyllis' ring. "I have more than eighty dollars now for it," said Hans, to Father Jim, "it's enough to get a cheaper ring that Phyllis and I were looking at, but I saw some that were a full carat, for $129. I would love to get her that, so she could have a good one, she'll have it for the rest of her life." "You say you have $83.19 now," said Father Jim, "with just a little more you should be able to get a ring that's almost a carat, she would be happy with whatever you give her, she knows how hard you are working to get the money for the ring." "I guess you're right, father," said Hans, "but it's a one-time thing, I want to show her how much I love her." "I think she knows that," said Father Jim. The weeks went on, and the mayor kept on with his weekly meeting about the latest war news. He had mostly good news, or nothing to report except for the continuing plans for the liberation of Europe. He did report the news of another one of the British ships sunk, with the loss of many sailors, but this was only rarely a part of his report, as the battle for the north Atlantic was being won by the Allies, and no casualties were reported from the Cross Bear area. Almost every week a German U-Boat and sometimes another ship, was reported sunk. The United States & other vessels were reaching England; the tide had turned in the longest battle of the war, the battle for the north Atlantic.

It was March, and Hans went to the church on the 4th for the choir's last get-together before Lent started on March 10th. They went over the usual songs to sing on Sunday, and also some songs for Ash Wednesday. Hans had borrowed Dan's truck for the rehearsal, so he stopped at the rectory afterward. But Father Jim had some bad news, something that was a bit frightening. "Sit down, Hans," said Father Jim, "I got a call from the FBI, they have been checking you out since you were away for the questioning, and they said they will be coming up to see you tomorrow, they asked me to tell you so you could be here, or at the town hall. They said that it was important for you to cooperate with them for this." "Well, of course I'll see them, if they have more questions, maybe it's something they forgot, before." "They sounded very serious, on the phone," said Father Jim. "You had better go to the ranch, and tell Dan that you have to be here. I'll come and get you, so it won't disturb the work."

"Thank you, father," said Hans, I'll go now and arrange for you to pick me up." "After lunch,' said Father Jim, "I know Dan will understand." "Oh, can I call Phyllis, to tell her?" said Hans, I want to inform her on what's going on, also." "Yes, go and call her, then get back to the ranch," said Father Jim. So Hans called Phyllis, and told her not to worry, though he knew she would. All the way back to the ranch Hans thought about what they wanted to talk to him about, that they hadn't already talked to him about. He thought for sure that they would have no more questions to ask him when he came home before. Hans would say his rosary before going to bed that night, it was time to put things in God's hands again, as he had before.

Chapter 16

Friday came, and Father Jim went up to the Blocker ranch to pick up Hans, after lunch. Hans got in the car saying, "The Blockers are worried about what the agents will be questioning me about, since they thought I was all done with any questioning." "Just answer them like before," said Father Jim, "it can't be any more than a minor thing that they need to know to close their case on you." "I hope you're right," said Hans. They then talked about what questions the agents might have, and finally decided that wasn't worth worrying about, they would again put it in God's hands.

At 1:20 a car pulled up in front of the rectory, and the same two agents who were with Hans before came to the front door. Marie welcomed them in, as she took their hats and coats. Father Jim and Hans met them, and the agents said they would need to talk in private. "We'll go to the living room," said Father Jim. Father Jim and Hans sat on the couch, with one of the agents, and the other FBI man sat in a chair, across from them. "I know you're wondering what we could have to ask you, after you went through all the other questions before,' said the agent on the chair, "I must tell you it's not good news. The FBI always does good background checks on anyone we question, as we did with you. We got your own fingerprints while you were with us, from a glass of water you drank from, your prints don't show up anywhere. That led us to check with all the prisons in the nation, since a few people don't have their fingerprints on record, until they go and break the law. We finally did a check with all prisoners of war, and got the report we had looked for from a prisoner of war camp in Oklahoma, about an alleged escapee. Not all the prisoners had been fingerprinted, and yours wasn't one of the ones they had. It wasn't until after the escape that the prison guards could check on the prisoners, after putting them in solitary, because of the escape, and some who rioted, that they could do a check to see who was there. They had thought they had caught all the escapees, but they realized that one named Hans Kruger wasn't there. They knew then that he had escaped, but that it had been a few days since the escape, and that it would be useless to try to find him now. So they finally just figured that some authorities would catch him somewhere, since he couldn't speak English." "But you do speak English," said the other FBI man, "so it helped us to believe you when we questioned you, since you spoke such good English." "But now," said the other agent, "we have to know, are you the one, the Hans Kruger who escaped from a prison in Oklahoma?" Hans looked at Father Jim, who nodded his head. "Yes, I am the escaped prisoner," said Hans, "but coming to America was the best thing that ever happened to me, it changed my way of thinking how Hitler's goals were wrong. I never wanted to be in the army, but any man out of high school, and even some still in high school, were taken into the military. And since I had taken a course in English in high school, they brought me to a place in north Africa where they were teaching me, and about a dozen others, to speak English, so that we could be used as spies in the United States, or in Britain. And I spoke English so well, without an accent, that they were planning to get me to a place in America, where I could get information from the Pentagon. But from the beginning, I didn't want to go to war, I don't think I could have killed another man or woman. That was why I wanted to become an American, why I wanted to be a citizen of this great country."

The two agents then stood up and went to the side of the room, and talked to each other about what Hans had said. "I think that what you said about wanting to become an American had an impression on them," said Father Jim. The agents came back to their seats, and the one sitting next to Hans said: "The fact that you're an American citizen speaks well for you. If you weren't, and we had even a slight suspicion that you were an escaped prisoner of war, things would be different. We wouldn't have notified you ahead of time. We would simply have come, with a guard, and arrested you, and then take you to a place for interrogation, and then to a prisoner of war camp, for the duration of the war. And if you denied anything about who you were, or gave us any trouble, we would have handcuffed you right away, before more extensive questioning first, in Lansing." "But you are a special case," said the other agent, "so we're going to tell about it when we report to the boss." "Who's the boss?" asked Hans. "They're talking about J. Edgar Hoover," said Father Jim, "he's the head of the Federal Bureau of Investigation, the FBI." "Yes," said the agent next to Hans, "the FBI keeps control of people, or businesses, that break the law, or do anything that threatens the security of the government. The SS in Germany does the same thing, but they are more ruthless in the way they do things. In America we still follow the law, and respect people's rights." "Your priest has it right," said the agent sitting in the chair, "what Hoover says, goes, the only one he answers to is the President of the United States of America. Hoover sometimes talks to Roosevelt about something, especially in a case like this. We'll be going back to the office now, and because you're a citizen we'll give you until Monday to come back to Lansing with us, we'll know, by then, what the answer will be from Hoover, or maybe from the President. We think you're a decent man. The fact that you went to the trouble of becoming a citizen speaks highly in your favor. But if Hoover says to put you back in prison, we'll have to do it." "So," said the agent sitting next to Hans, "use the time from now until we come back Monday to take care of things, in case you are sent back to prison. "We know you are planning on getting married to Phyllis Thaxter, have you set a date for the wedding?" "No, we were just about to get together about that," said Hans. "You'll need to postpone your wedding for now, and talk to Miss Thaxter about you going away, but you can't talk about any of the details," said the agent in the chair. "We don't know ourselves what will be happening, but we'll fill you in when we come for you on Monday. Also, you took out a three year loan to buy your house. If you're gone, you wouldn't be able to make the payments, do you think Miss Thaxter could make them for you for the rest of the three years of the loan?" "I think she could," said Hans, "since she wouldn't need to set any money aside, for now, for our wedding." "But there would be a problem, if you're in prison," said the agent sitting on the couch, "if you are a prisoner of war, you couldn't own any property in the United States. When Phyllis made the last payment, the house would go to the county, or the state, however the law has it. Your years of paying the loan would be for no purpose. There's one way out of this, just in case. You can't change the loan, that's in your name, but you could change the property over to Phyllis' name, so that even if you were a prisoner of war, the house would belong to her, so that you and she could work things out from there. Get a lawyer who knows how to do it, and have the deed put in your intended's name, that way you won't lose the property. When you come back, you can have the property changed back into your name, unless you just wait until you are married, and can then have it changed into both your names, if you wish. But you will need to get it done before we come to get you." "We'll spend the weekend with talking to Hoover, and explain the situation," said the agent in the chair, Hoover will probably call the President for his opinion, but most of the time Roosevelt leaves it up to Hoover to do what he thinks best. But you can't tell Phyllis anything about what's going on, since she isn't your wife. We'll pass on any word about what happens to Father O'Connell, we know he can be trusted to keep things confidential. Is that right, father?" said the agent. "Oh yes," said Father Jim, "I'm in the business for confidentiality." "Well, we have to go now," said the senior agent. We'll see you on Monday, Hans. Remember what I said about getting a lawyer, and changing the deed." "Yes, we'll do that," said Father Jim. "And I'll do anything I can, to help Hans."

"We're in Hans' corner, too," said the other agent, "but we can't guarantee anything." The agents left to go back to Lansing, a ferry had already been assigned to get them to the lower part of the state. They knew they had their work cut out for them, with Hoover.

Father Jim started making plans with Hans for what they must do to get a legal transfer of the property. "I'm going to get ahold of Mickey Roney. He's just a farmer, raises pigs, but he's also licensed attorney, who makes some spare money by doing legal work, once in a while," said Father Jim. He did some work for us two years ago, to settle the border of the land of the rectory, and the house next to us. He's not Catholic, but he does good legal work. He has a neighbor, Peter Lorie, who takes care of his farm if Mickey is busy on a case for 2 or 3 days. I'll have to drive out to Mickey's farm to tell him that we need him, he doesn't have a telephone."

So Father Jim and Hans went to the Roney farm, to make sure they could get him at home before Monday, so he could do what he had to for the property transfer. When they got there, Father Jim saw Peter Lorie just leaving, as Mickey had just returned from a case of a man accused of horse stealing, out of town. "Hello, Mister Roney," said Father Jim, as he introduced Hans, "Oh yes, I recall, I helped settle a boundary dispute with you, for your church, I forget the name," said Mickey. "My church is Good Shepherd Church," said Father Jim, "I'm coming to you this time to change the name on a deed." "Well, I just got back, let me get settled, to make sure everything's all right here," said Mickey, I can see you sometime on Monday, in the afternoon, to get things started with the town hall, we have to do this through there, and they're closed for the weekend." "But it can be opened for an emergency," said Father Jim.

"This thing has to be done by noon on Monday, or by 1 o'clock." "Well, I'm willing, but the town hall, where all the town records are kept, including deeds," said Mickey. "I know the mayor will be willing to meet us there," said Father Jim. "Well, when do you want me there?" said the lawyer. "I'll stop by the mayor's house on the way back, I'll have him open up the town hall by 11 o'clock," said Father Jim. "Meet with us there then. I think he'll need his secretary for this, also, the mayor doesn't know the details about the paperwork involved for this," said Father Jim. "But I charge an extra $5 for doing this on the weekend," said Mickey. "We'll pay it," said Father Jim, and Hans, in unison. "My fee is $15, but for a return customer, it's just $12," said Mickey. "That's fine, I'll have the $17 for you tomorrow," said Father Jim. "But I want to pay for it." said Hans. "We'll both pay," said Father Jim, "I'll pay $!0, I can bring that out of our emergency fund. You bring the $7," said Father Jim. "All right, but I will pay back $5 to the emergency fund," said Hans. "We'll work those things out later,' said Father Jim, "We'll see you at 11 o'clock tomorrow at town hall," said Father Jim, to Mickey. "I'll be there," said Mickey Roney.

So Father Jim and Hans stopped by the mayor's house, it was a little bit after 6 o'clock, supper time. Robert answered the door. "I have to talk with you about opening up town hall tomorrow morning,' said Father Jim. "Oh, I'm sorry, you're just sitting down for supper, we can wait, and talk to you after." "Who is it?" said Robert's wife, "Oh, hello, father, won't you stay for supper?" "Oh no, we didn't come for that," said Father Jim. "Come, I have a nice fish dinner, it was caught this morning, some of it," said Mrs. Horton. "Well, I guess we can settle it after supper," said Father Jim, "but I have to call Marie, to let her know that I won't be there." "Of course," said Robert, "there's the phone." So Father Jim called Marie, and settled down for a nice supper with the mayor's family.

At 11 o'clock on the next morning Father Jim and Hans met with the mayor, as he opened up the town hall. Mickey Roney then came to start the legal part of changing the deed. "I called in my part time secretary," said the mayor, "my regular secretary wouldn't come in on Saturday, unless I had a gun to her head. Father, this is Gloria Talbot, she knows where things are, and what to do. She fills in when my regular secretary is sick, or on vacation." So Gloria got the necessary papers for a new deed, and had both Hans and Mickey sign for them. Hans then gave Mickey the $17 for their deal, and the lawyer left to go home and type up the papers for signing, on Monday. He told Hans to make sure Phyllis was there for the signing.

After Mass, the next morning, Hans took Phyllis over to the rectory for breakfast, and then took her to the living room and sat down on the nice couch with her. "I'll be going away Monday," said Hans, with the agents who were with me before. There's no guarantee I'll be back for a while, I'll know what the story is when they come. But they advised me to have the deed to the house changed over to you, just in case." "Just in case of what?" said Phyllis, "Hans, you're scaring me." "I'm sorry, but I don't know exactly what is going on yet, I'll find out Monday," said Hans, "I can't tell you what it is because you're not my wife." "But we were going to get together to plan our date," said Phyllis. "I know, said Hans, "but we'll have to put those plans off for now. We will get married, someday. All you need to know now is that we need to get the deed changed into your name. We'll be meeting with the attorney tomorrow at the Roney farm, to sign the papers, you have to come, to sign the papers." "But what about the loan payments?" asked Phyllis. "it will be all right, since you won't need to put anything aside for the wedding for a while," said Hans, "you can make them, until I return. Father Jim is the only one who will know what is happening, he'll tell you what's going on, if he can, he's the only one the agents will trust with whatever's happening. You'll know everything, eventually." "All right," said Phyllis, "if I'm going to be your wife, I need to trust you, and I do" Hans then kissed his loving, and worried, future wife, and hugged her as he said; "That's all I need to know, sweetheart." Then Father Jim came in to see how Phyllis was taking the news. "Oh, I'm sorry, I can come back," said Father Jim. "Oh, that's all right," said Phyllis, as she left Hans and took Father Jim's hand, "I know that you will be the only one the agents will be talking to." "Yes, and I won't know what that will be until I meet with them tomorrow," said Father Jim, "but I'll tell you everything I can." Phyllis then hugged her pastor, and said; "Thank you, father, I know I can trust you." "But we need you tomorrow, for the signing of the deed," said Father Jim. "I know," said Phyllis, "I'll get off work, my boss will understand." "We'll pick you up a little before ten, on our way to the farm," said Father Jim. "I'll be waiting," said Phyllis. Father Jim then left Hans and Phyllis, so they could be together for a while, before going to his bedroom, to say some special prayers for Hans and Phyllis.

The next day Father Jim and Hans picked up Phyllis at home, to take her to the Roney farm. "Welcome, come in," said Mickey Roney as he escorted everyone to his dining room table. "I have the papers all ready for signing," said Mickey, as everyone sat down at the table. Mickey then explained what each part of the transfer meant, then he had Hans sign, as the current owner, and had Phyllis sign, as the new owner, and then, in another place, affirming that she understood the terms of the transfer. Then Father Jim signed, as a witness. Then he signed the place for the attorney. Then, as he took the papers apart he took out two pieces of black paper. "You see these?" said Mickey, they're used so you don't have to sign papers 3, or 4 times. I hear that many secretaries use them now, this is the first time I've used them. They're called carbon papers. The first copy here is what I'll keep, for my records, and in case anything happens to the first paper. The second copy goes to the new owner, said Mickey, as he handed it to Phyllis. The top one you'll take to the town secretary. See this line below my signature? That's where the secretary will sign and date it, & then put it with the other town records, and remove the old deed, which she'll put in a place they have for old papers. It will be official then, Miss Thaxter. Say, I've seen the property, it goes out into the country a way, you must have at least two acres there." "I've checked it," said Hans, "it's a little over three acres." "That's enough to have a small herd of cattle, or something," said Mickey. "Yes, I had that in mind," said Hans. "If we're all done," said Phyllis, "I need to get back to the diner. It's lunch time, my boss will have a hard time handling things, without me." "We'll take you right there," said Father Jim, "then we'll take the new deed to town hall and get it to the secretary."

So they dropped Phyllis off at the Turner Diner, where Abagail was eagerly waiting for her waitress, and part time cook. Then they went to the town hall, and the secretary did her job, it was all done now, nice and legal. Then Father Jim and Hans went to the rectory for lunch, and then waited for the two agents to come. Hans had already packed a small bag to take, with about a third of his clothes in it.

About 2:15 a car pulled up in front of the rectory, Father Jim saw it was the FBI men. Then the agents got out of the car, and came up to the front porch. Father Jim opened the door and welcomed them in. "Hello," said Marie, as she also came to greet them, "would you like a cup of hot coffee?" "No thanks," said the first agent, "we had some in a diner, after we got off the ferry. "Well, if you want anything, just let me know," said Marie, as she went into the kitchen. The two agents then sat down on the couch, with Hans sitting between them, and Father Jim sat on a chair near them, where he was ready to speak up on Hans' behalf.

"It's good news!" said the senior agent, "you won't have to be sent back to prison, for the rest of the war." "Just what are you saying?" asked Father Jim. "We spent all weekend working on this," said the other agent, "we called Hoover, explained the situation, and he said he would have to get back to us, after calling the President. After about an hour and a half Hoover got back to us, and said that we could handle the situation as we had planned. But when Roosevelt was told about Hans being a citizen, he said that he would pardon Hans from any prisoner of war charges." "Is it true?" said Hans. "Yes," said the first agent, "if you were just a prisoner of war, we would've had to send you to a POW camp for the duration of the war. But since you are a citizen, Roosevelt could pardon you." "Did you really mean it when you said you would do anything to help our country, when you were questioned before?" asked the other agent. "Yes, I said that several times," said Hans. "Well, here's your chance to really do it," said the other agent, "by helping us to get information for our military." "How can I do that?" asked Hans. "You were trained to be a spy, now you can do it for us. You see, we have agents in France, and Germany, but they have a hard time getting information to us, and the ones who are caught pay the price for espionage. The French underground helps some, but is hindered by the German SS forces." "We'll give you a week of training," said the other agent, "for your protection, and teach you how to find out information from some of the German officers we have in our prisons. The things we need to know most are where Germany has its underground factories, and where the Germans have their stashes of weapons, mostly in northern France, and Belgium. These will be used to reinforce their troops, in the case of an Allied invasion. Our forces have fought off the Luftwaffe, to the point where we can send bombers over the occupied territories, & as far as Germany, soon. If our military knows where these factories, & weapon stockpiles are, we can bomb them, and weaken Germany, and shorten the war, with many less lives lost, on both sides. We know that 8 of our prisoner of war camps have some of the higher German officers, who know where the places we want to know of are. These are the camps we'll send you to, for a two week period. The job should be over in four months." "That's wonderful," said Hans, "because I have a pretty girl who's waiting to marry me." "We know all about Miss Thaxter," said the second agent, "we've checked her out." "But she hasn't done anything," said Hans. "We know, but we have to check out in depth anyone who is associated with you, before we can give you a job like this," said the first agent." "Don't worry, everything is fine with your girl," said the second agent. "But you can't say anything to her about what you're doing, word could get to a German spy somewhere." "And there's a good part to this," said the senior agent, "you'll be paid for the work you'll be doing. We have a special fund for espionage agents, since it's so important, and often dangerous.

We pay up to $100 a week for some in such places as Berlin, or Tokyo. All men who do this are volunteers, from the army, we don't order anyone to do this, a dangerous job. You'll have to join the army, in order to do this, it will just be on a temporary basis, until the job is done. Then you'll be discharged, and will be a veteran. Oh, we'll pay you $50 a week, for the 4 months of work, after a week's training Two of the main trainers are Jay Silverheels and Zebedie Titus, along with three others for special parts of training. Dan Dureay will be with you for one day, maybe two, to teach you to correspond with codes we use for our messages. If the message falls into the wrong hands, they won't know what it says. But when you get it to one of our agents, just outside the prison, we'll decode it, and pass on the information to the military. A woman named Madelyn Rue will check you in to our special training quarters, a guard will frisk you for weapons; it's all part of the standard operating procedure. Everyone going in to our facility is checked this way, except us two, and the head of our office in Lansing. You'll get used to it." "Oh, the $50 a week," said the second agent, "we can't send it to you, you'll be too busy with your job. But we can send it to Father O'Connell, made out to him, so he can cash it, and give the money to your girl, to take care of your loan, or put it in your bank account, or use it for other things, until you return." "I'll do it," said Father Jim. "Well, I think that's about it," said the junior agent, "you can write your Phyllis a message telling her that you'll be gone for 4 months, but that you can't say what you're doing. If there are no more questions, we'll be on to Lansing, to start your training tomorrow. But first, write your girl a message. "We'll have to read it," said the senior agent, "to make sure nothing you say will give away the nature of your job." "I understand," said Hans, I'll write it now." Hans had a lot to think about as he wrote, but he finally put the pen to paper, and thought about what he should say to the woman who loved and trusted him, and would be very upset by his absence in her life, since she was so used to him being there. So he thought deeply, and wrote.

My darling, I'll be gone for a while, in the service of my country. It's a special case, and they'll be paying me $50 a week, after training, which will be sent to Father Jim. He'll cash it, and give the money to you. Here's what I want you to do with it. For the first 2 weeks, make 2 advance payments on the loan. Then, from the 3rd week on, make one advance payment, & use the rest for the house, or whatever else you need it for. Since you won't need to use your own pay for much else, put $5 into the collection each week, while I'm away. I might not be able to go to Mass while I'm on assignment, but I'll still be praying for you, I know you'll be praying for me. So, mind the store while I'm gone, and you just remember one thing – when I get back, I'm going to marry you.

Love, Hans

Hans looked it over to make sure he didn't leave anything out, and gave it to the agents, who took the paper as it was given to them, and read it carefully, nodding their heads as they read. "It's all right,' said the senior agent, "it's very sweet. I hope she realizes what a wonderful husband she'll be getting, not that she isn't a wonderful girl, also." The agent then gave the letter to Father Jim, and said to give it to Miss Thaxter as soon as he could, & tell her to put it away somewhere, just to be on the safe side. A woman who handles our proofreading, Virginia Gray, would love to read this." "Well, we had better get going," said the senior agent, "we'd like to catch the ferry by 5 o'clock, if we're going to get back to Lansing before ten. Hans then hugged Father Jim, who told him that he would be praying for him. Hans then went to the kitchen to say goodbye to Marie. Marie hugged Hans, and kissed him on the cheek. "You take care of yourself," said Marie, "oh, I wish you didn't have to go away from us." "But I do have to," said Hans, "I'll be back before long, you can't get rid of me that easily." Hans then picked up his bag with some of his clothes in it, just enough for a few days, since he was sure the FBI would be supplying him with other clothes. The agents still had to inspect his bag. When they found nothing but clothes, a pair of slippers, and shaving gear, they gave it back to him. "I know, it's just SOP," said Hans. He was beginning to get used to the security which the FBI had to operate with. The two agents walked with Hans to the car, as Father Jim and Marie looked on from the porch, with Marie starting to cry again, as she waved goodbye to Hans.

So, things were set for Hans, as he was headed for the biggest, and very possibly, most dangerous adventure of his life, as he would be living with men who would, without hesitating, end his short life, if they found out who he was, or what he was doing. But he also thought of the wonderful reward that would await him, when he finally returned home, to the woman he loved. Hans was looking out of the window, as he asked the agents about the dangers of his job, and about what he would be learning in his week of training. They told him that all his questions would be answered, during his week of training. "It should be a bit easier for you than others trained," said the senior agent, "since you have already been through this kind of training before, with your German agents." "I suppose," said Hans, "but I know that this will be different, because the men I was trained with in north Africa also taught us how to kill, with no hesitation, if someone found out who we were, even if it was a woman or a child." "I think you know that we're not that cold – blooded," said the other agent. "Some of our men who are spying for us do have to kill sometimes, to stay alive. But this won't be the same with you. The men you'll be with won't be armed, as a rule, but you'll be taught what to do to disarm a man with a knife, or gun." "All of our men who are in the army go through that in basic training, and you will be, just for now, a member of the army," said the other agent. They reached the ferry, and Hans spent most of the time praying to his God to guide him, and protect him on this dangerous journey he was taking, for his sake, and for the ones he loved.

Chapter 17

After a while Father Jim had Marie comforted, with Marie acting as if she would never see Hans again. Father Jim said that he was going to say a rosary for Hans' safety, then some private prayers. Marie composed herself, then also said some prayers, before going to the kitchen to fix supper. After supper Marie told Father Jim that she was going to her room to say a rosary for Hans. Father Jim listened to the radio until 7:30, and then got the letter Hans wrote for Phyllis, and got in the car to go to the diner, to give the letter to Phyllis.

Father Jim got to the diner about 7:50, ten minutes before closing time. There was one last late supper person at a table, who was just getting up from the chair, and going over to Abagail, to pay his bill, as Phyllis came out to clear the table. "Oh, hello, father," said Phyllis, as she spotted her pastor coming in the door, "we close in a few minutes." "I'm not here to eat, I came to see you about something," said Father Jim. "All right, I just have to take these dishes into the kitchen to be washed, before I call my mother to come and get me. I could walk, it's just a few blocks, but my mom says a girl shouldn't walk the streets at night," said Phyllis. "Well, you listen to your mother," said Father Jim, "but I can give you a ride home, as soon as you're done here." So, after taking the last tray to the kitchen for washing, Phyllis asked her boss if the pastor could stay for a few minutes, and talk to her pastor. "Yes, said Miss Turner, as she saw Father Jim sitting at one of the tables. "But I'm leaving now, you'll have to lock up." "I will," said Phyllis, as she came over to Father Jim and sat at the table with him. "I'm afraid I have bad news for you," said Father Jim. "About Hans?" asked Phyllis. "Yes," continued Father Jim. "You knew about us meeting with the FBI agents? Well, we did, and this is what happened. Hans has been freed of any charges as a prisoner of war, but he's been asked to do something to help our war effort. So, he left this afternoon about 3 o'clock with the FBI agents, he'll be on a voluntary assignment, away from here, for about four months, after a week of training."

"Training?" said Phyllis, "for what?" asked a frightened Phyllis. "I can't tell you that,' said her pastor, "I'm the only one they are confiding in, I can't tell anyone else, not even you." "But I don't understand" – said Phyllis. "I know, you're upset, but what he's doing is so important that they're paying him." said Father Jim, as he tried to speak in a soothing voice. "They let Hans write you a letter that can explain some of it, as he handed her the letter Hans had written. Then Phyllis took the letter, and slowly read it. Her eyes started watering as she read each sentence. Then, when she read the last sentence, where Hans told her that he would marry her, she burst into tears, stood up, and gave Father Jim a hug. Father Jim did his best to calm Phyllis, as he said, "It's all right, it's a nice letter that he wrote you, and it shows how much he loves you. We will all miss him, but he'll be back after four months, when he has had a week of training, first. He's doing this job for his country, but he's really doing it for you, honey." Phyllis then looked at the letter again, which had several of Phyllis' tears on it, then said: "Yes, I'll make the advance payments for the loan, and I'll "mind the store" by doing whatever else I can here, for our house, until my Hans returns. I know he's doing a task that's dangerous, but I know our Lord will look after him." "Yes," said Father Jim, and on Sunday I'll tell our people that Hans had to leave us for a while, and that we should pray for him." Then Father Jim took a somewhat shaken Phyllis home, where she gave Father Jim another hug, then went in to tell her parents of what Hans was doing.

Back in Lansing the two agents and Hans came to the building that Hans had been in before for questioning. They stopped there, then handed Hans a black blindfold, and Hans put it on. Then they drove on, making a few turns, for about three minutes, before stopping, and taking his blindfold off. They were in front of a building, one with bars on the windows. They walked in the front door, into a room with a desk, with a woman sitting at it, with a guard standing nearby. "This is Melanie Craig, she's the night secretary who I told you about, she's on from 6 until 11 PM, when the building is closed. A different woman will be checking you in, for each day," said the senior agent.

"Melanie, this is Hans Kruger", said the agent, to the secretary, "I'm just going to show him some of the rooms he'll be going to." The guard took a step toward Hans, but the agent said: "It's all right, he's with us." The man stepped back to his original spot. "That's Frank Avalon," said the agent, one of our night guards. Another guard will greet you, and frisk you, as you check in, in the morning. It's their job to frisk anyone who comes into this facility, except for us, the five men who will be doing the training, and, of course, our pretty secretaries," said the agent, as he looked toward the desk, where a girl named Melanie smiled, and nodded her head in appreciation, for the compliment. "It's just SOP, as we call it, but it is necessary, especially since Pearl Harbor. "Now, we'll show you some of the rooms for a few minutes." said the first agent. Then Hans was shown some rooms with tables and chairs, and a room with some weapons, and some maps that looked like those from prison camps. He was then taken out, and led to a small cabin, where he was to sleep, and spend some time for studying the things they would teach him. "When you get up, around 8 AM,' said the agent, "you'll go to the diner you see across the street for breakfast, everything's paid for. A guard will escort you to the diner, and then to the training building. You'll get used to the body checking before you go to the rooms. Until I rose to the position I have now, I went through it too. It's just…" "I know," said Hans, "just SOP."

So Hans spent the night in the cabin, on a bed that was pretty soft, and warm. Unknown to him, a guard was stationed just outside the front door, as part of the security of this place. An alarm clock was there, on a small table by the bed, and Hans set it for 7:45. He awoke to the alarm, ringing, and shut off the alarm. Then he washed, shaved, dressed, and went out the front door, and a guard went with him to the diner, where they both had breakfast. Then he was given a bag lunch, so that he could stay in the building until his trainings were finished, around 5, or 5:30. As he and the guard went into the building he saw another secretary sitting at the desk. She asked his name, and marked him off on a list she had. Then the guard who was in the office came, and did his job of frisking him, then told him to go in. One of the trainers met him, and took him to a room to begin training. He gave him an overview of what they would be teaching him, then started in with the first lesson.

As the days went by, most of what they taught him was what he had learned in north Africa. But it took him almost three days to learn lessons in how to write a message in code, they had 4 different codes to teach him. He finally had them all down, good enough to suit the trainers, so that he was ready to start his job. He was now ready to be given prison garb to wear, so he would fit in with the prisoners in the 8 prisons they had him scheduled to go to, on his espionage mission.

Hans did good with this undercover job, as he didn't have any trouble blending in with the prisoners, and in a few days getting to know the higher officers who were there, who knew of the places Hans had to find out, and get to an agent outside the prison, in code. He had to remember the name he was given, and not to say anything in English, and to act as if he didn't understand it if a guard, or anyone else spoke in English. He didn't see many Japanese prisoners, with only a few Italians.

As the weeks went by, Hans didn't find out anything in two of the POW camps he was in, but in the other six he found out where several underground factories were, and a few of the munitions stashes locations, as well. The FBI would pass on this information to the military, which would be successful in bombing the sites, in the weeks to come, destroying some factories, and also some weapons supply dumps, that would be of no help to Germany when the Allies did come to take back Europe from Hitler.

Meanwhile, back at the ranch, so to speak, Phyllis did as Hans had told her. She made the advance payments on the loan, coming back with 50 cents, after Father Jim gave her the $50 for the job Hans was doing. Since she didn't have to worry about the loan, she used most of the money from her job for getting some inexpensive things for the house. When the older couple left, they left silverware in a drawer, next to the sink, enough for five or six people, of different patterns. Phyllis already had plans for having a dinner for about 10 or 12 people, for a Thanksgiving or Christmas meal, so she took money she had from her pay at the diner, and bought a set of silverware for 6, and added a set for 2 she had in her room, & added them to the ones the couple had left. They didn't all match, but some of them did. She now had enough for about eleven people. On the third week that Father Jim gave her the $50, she paid another advance payment on the loan, and put the other $25 into her savings account, which she had started right after she started working in the diner, with fifty cents. As often as she could she added a dollar, or another fifty cents, and she had more than $!4 in it, but now had almost $40 in it. She thought that she and Hans would need a car after they got married, to go to places, instead of asking others to borrow their truck, car, or horse. She promised herself to put $10 into the account each week, to eventually buy a car, and use the rest for things for the house. She knew that the car dealer in town had several used cars, ones from 1925 to 1934, with two newer ones that two people had traded in for a new 1942 car, the last ones the dealer had, as new cars were harder to get a deal from, with the auto dealers using most of their machinery for making many weapons for the war. The cheapest car had a $34 price on it, but was not in good enough shape to last more than 2 years. The others ranged from $39 to $79, but only the 1934 Buick was in good enough condition to last for more than 3 or 4 years. The newest ones, a 1938 Buick, & a 1939 Chevrolet, were priced at $147, and $158, and were in good condition. With almost $40 in her account, Phyllis vowed to save enough for one of the two newest cars, especially the 1939 one, it would last for at least 6 years.

But other things were on Phyllis' list of things for the house. She had enough silverware now, but she needed more dishes, as the two people who used to live there only left enough dishes for 3 or 4 people. So, one week the enterprising waitress took part of the extra $25 to get a new set of dishes, one for 6 people, for $16. She now had enough dishes for 10 or 11 people. Next, she wanted to replace the small table in the kitchen with a table large enough for 10 or 12 people, for a Thanksgiving or Christmas dinner. But she heard of a young family who had one child, and another on the way, with a small table that was falling apart, so she had them come and get the one she had in her kitchen, it would be fine for them, until they had some more kids, at least. She then used some of the extra money from Hans, and her own money, to buy a table large enough for 10, maybe 12 people, with an understanding that the store people would bring it to her house, and set it in her large room, near the kitchen. This would make the large room a combined dining room/ living room, which would make a nice entranceway into the house, for when friends or relatives came to be with her and Hans.

One day Father Jim stopped at the diner on his way back from a visit at a house that had been partly burned, the year before, after which the people who had lived in it moved away, since they didn't have the money to rebuild it. Father Jim stopped to have a cup of coffee and a piece of apple pie, and to see Phyllis. Since it was mid afternoon, he knew she wouldn't be busy. "Hello Phyllis," said Father Jim, "I'll have a cup of coffee and a piece of apple pie." "Sure, said Phyllis, "as soon as I take this last tray of dishes to the kitchen. It's so nice to see you again." Phyllis then told her boss that she wanted to talk to her pastor for a few minutes, as she poured a cup of coffee, and put a slice of apple pie on a dish, to take to Father Jim. It's so nice to see you stop by," said Phyllis, as she placed the cup of coffee and the apple pie down, and sat with him, and took a sip from the cup of coffee she poured for herself. "I just came from a home that was half burned down," said Father Jim, "a new older couple just moved in." "I didn't hear of a house burning," said Phyllis. "Oh, it happened more than a year ago, before you came here, a little before Christmas," said Father Jim, the couple who lived there were parishioners, they left for Wisconsin, and left the house to me, to see if our church members could fix it up so that it could be lived in again. We had some money set aside in a building fund, so we used some of it to buy wood and have the burned part of the house torn down, and built it up again with siding, & replaced the burned part of the roof. Six of our parishioners volunteered their time and efforts to do this, as a few others helped out. The bedroom was burned some with the left side of the mattress on the bed burned. They had everything else repaired, but never got around to getting a new mattress. An older couple moved here from the eastern part of the peninsula, and they didn't have enough money to buy a house, so I gave it to them. Since half of the bed wasn't burned, the man let his wife sleep on the unburned half, and he slept in a chair." "Oh, my gosh, that is not right," said Phyllis. "They would need a double sized mattress to replace it," said Father Jim. "Tell them to take it to the dump," said Phyllis, "they can have the mattress in my house, I won't need one for a while, I'll get another one for me later. It's a few years old, but it's in good condition, and it's a double sized mattress. They can have it, a man & his wife should sleep in the same bed." "That's fine," said Father Jim. "Are you sure you'll be all right without it?" "I won't be sleeping there for a while," said Phyllis, "I'll use the extra money to get a mattress for Hans and me some time. " "You're doing a great job, getting the things you need for the house," said Father Jim, "I heard about the big table you got for a big dinner." "Yes, it will seat 10, maybe 12 people,' said Phyllis, "I had only 4 chairs in the house, but the store where I got the table also has chairs, so I got a set of 4 nice ones, made by a local carpenter. His store had them priced at $4 each, or 4 for $15. I told the store owner to get 4 more, and I would buy them, too. Then I'll have enough chairs to go with the big table. I'll also get a small couch someone has for sale, for the living room, and put a couple of the chairs by it, with a small table I got for $2, for meeting with others, and maybe putting coffee, or other thing son it, for 5 or 6 people. And the old couple only had a few pots and pans, so I got some others, and other cooking utensils, for cooking up a big dinner." "Hans will be proud of you," said Father Jim, "for the things you've done here, when he gets back," said Father Jim, "but some people are beginning to wonder about where you're getting the money to buy all these things, including the bank people, when you come in each week to make a payment." "That's just between us," said Phyllis. "And the last thing I'll get for our house is an electric refrigerator. They aren't always available, but I put an order in for one from the general store's Sears catalogue. I don't think more than 10 or 12 people have one, but once I get the electric hooked up, we won't have to worry if the ice man can't make it this week, especially in the summer." "Yes, you really are "minding the store"," said Father Jim, as he sipped his coffee.

Phyllis left Father Jim. To do what she had planned, for the next three months of Han's time with the government. Hans was planning, also, for his lifetime with Phyllis, and also for the ring he would be getting her. They had looked at rings, most of them were about half of a carat, for $50 to $65. The extra jobs Hans had done while still working on the ranch, and the farm, and for a few others, had been his source of saving for it. There was a ring, a one carat ring, that was $127, and he had saved $130 before he went away to do his job for the government. But he wanted to get one that was about a carat and a half, for $179, even though Phyllis had said that she would be happy as could be with a half carat ring, if it was from Hans.

Meanwhile, Phyllis had purchased a new mattress to replace the one she had given to the older couple in the formerly burned out house, and had followed Hans' idea of having the man who made the dresser he gave to Cora and Andrew for a wedding present, for their bedroom. It was the same size, but was made out of maple, it was $12 cheaper than a walnut one. Then she was told the refrigerator was in, so she took a little out of her auto savings to pay for it, and have a man from the store help her to put it in the kitchen. She would replace the borrowed money the next week, for her car fund. By now all the improvements to the house had increased the value of the house to about $900. And, with the roughly three acres of land and small barn being worth at least $600, the home they had bought for $1,000 was worth at least $1,500, before cattle were purchased for raising, if Hans were to ever sell it.

Then, the weeks had gone by quickly for Hans, even though he was on guard always to make sure he wasn't discovered by the prisoners. As he found out some more information last week that confirmed some that he had been able to come up with earlier, and sent out to an FBI agent, with the last bit of information about a new weapons supply stash, in some places in the occupied nation of Belgium, in his last week. He then brought the information with him, as the FBI had him moved from the camp for the last time, as he had completed a temporary job with the army. The army colonel in charge of this information assignment welcomed Hans back, and had him get washed and shaved, before being given his own clothes back, in place of the prisoner's garb he had been wearing. "The check for your last week's work has already been mailed," said the colonel, "your Father O'Connell should have it by now. And I said that you should get a $50 bonus for the job you did, but the army said no. They would only get $50 for each week you were in the army. So I told them that you were technically in the army when you had your week of training, so they relented, and I have a check for you for that week, made out to you, take it back with you, you can use it for whatever you wish, maybe for your house, or for the lady you'll be marrying." Hans thanked the colonel, and was then given an honorable discharge from the army, and then given a man to drive him back home, back to his church. "Corporal Klinger will take you back," said the colonel, "we thank you very much for the information you have given us, it will serve to shorten this bloody war."

So the corporal drove Hans back home, to the rectory, with a nice talk with the corporal about Han's experiences in the POW camps, and his success in carrying out his mission, and also about how pretty his girl was. The army had called Father Jim, to let him know that Hans had completed his mission, and that he would be coming home today. Father Jim had just the day before received the last $50 check he would be getting, and Phyllis had the money now, to make one more advance payment on the loan, and to get a few last items for the kitchen.

After what seemed like a long trip, Hans was dropped off at the church rectory, with Father Jim and Marie there to welcome him, along with Dan Blocker, the mayor, Father Salva, and a few members of the choir. "Oh, I'm so glad to be back," said Hans, "it's been a miserable four months, but the job is a success, and the potential danger of the job is over." "You don't know how much we've missed you," said Marie, as she hugged him, and started to cry again. "Oh Father," said Hans, "I need to go to confession as soon as I can, I didn't have a chance to go to Mass while I was gone, not even for Easter, because of where I was." "I'm sure the Lord will understand," said Father Jim. "Yes, the Lord is forgiving," said Hans, "but I still won't feel right in receiving the Holy Eucharist, until I go to confession. Oh, I thought Phyllis would be here, did anyone tell her I was coming home?" "She had to go in for work today," said Father Jim, "the woman who usually works Friday couldn't come in. She says she'll meet you after work." "All right, but then I'll go to see Dan at the ranch," said Hans, "he wants to have me back to work again. The others have been working longer hours, with me gone, but now I want to go and see the Zerbees." Father Jim then said he would take him there, and then to see Phyllis. Hans thanked him, and got in the car, after one more hug from Marie.

At the Zerbee farm Hans went to the main house, everyone was there to greet him. The women gave him a kiss and a hug, the men gave him a quick hug, and a welcome home greeting. They all questioned him about his job, & how he managed to do it. Then Cora took Hans to the side, and said: "I've been keeping in touch with Phyllis each week, wait until you see what she's done at your house! She really loves you, Hans." "Tell me something I don't Know," said Hans, as he gave Cora another hug.

About 8 o'clock Father Jim drove Hans to the Thaxter home, and Phyllis was waiting. Hans didn't get to the front door, as Phyllis opened it and met her loved one with a long kiss, and a hug. "Oh, I'm so glad you're back," said Phyllis, as she kissed him again. They then went into the house, where Phyllis' mother gave Hans a hug, and a kiss on the cheek, as her father shook his hand, and welcomed his back. "I got the afternoon off tomorrow," said Phyllis, "I want you to see what your house looks like." "You mean your house, don't you?" asked Hans. "I mean our house," said Phyllis, as she gave Hans another kiss, and hug. "I'll be done about 1:30," said Phyllis, "my boss said she can handle things from then on, as she isn't as busy on Saturday." "I have to go and see Dan now," said Hans, to see how soon I have to get back to work, I'll tell him that I need the weekend off, to get caught up with things." "I'm sure he will let you, after what you have been through," said Phyllis. "Well, I'll see you at 1:30 tomorrow," said Hans, as he walked out the front door. Then Phyllis said, loudly, "HEY!! Hans stopped, turned around, and walked to Phyllis to give her a goodbye kiss, then left. Phyllis' mother was standing nearby, and said to her daughter, "Well, it looks like you've got him trained." "Oh no, mom," said Phyllis, "a man like Hans will never be "trained", as you put it. I just want to make sure he still loves me." "I don't think you have to worry about that," said her mother, as she put her arms around her happy daughter.

At the ranch Hans said he would need the weekend off, to get caught up with things. He also said that he would need some time off Monday, or on Tuesday morning, to take care of something for Phyllis. "I'll be in the fields on Monday morning, working with the others on the fences," said Dan, "you can take the truck, just get back as soon as you can, I have some things for you to do, also." Hans thanked Dan, who said that he understood, that he was young and in love too, a few years back.

The next morning Hans took one of the horses from the ranch, went to the rectory, so that he could go to Father Jim to say his confession. After, he had a talk with Father Jim and Marie about the job he had done, then asked Father Jim if he could take the car so he could go with Phyllis, to go and see the house, for the first time since he had been gone. "Phyllis has things to show me," said Hans. "Yes, you can be proud of what that girl has done," said Father Jim. So Hans drove the car out to the diner, where Phyllis was just finishing with some of the last lunch dishes. "Go ahead," said Abagail, "I'll finish up", she said, as she saw Hans and waved to him. "You'll be all right for the supper?" asked Phyllis. "Yes, remember how I told you how I was doing everything by myself, until I hired you?" said Miss Turner. So Phyllis took off her apron, and went to greet Hans with her usual kiss and hug.

On the way to the house Phyllis said, "You'll like what I've done with the house, the things I've done while you were gone." "Yes, Cora has told me that I would like the house." Said Hans. "Oh," said Phyllis, Cora told me what they're going to name their baby." "But, they don't know yet...." said Hans. "If it's a boy, they're going to name him Matthew, after a disciple, and also after our bishop, but his middle name will be Hans," said Phyllis. "Oh? And..." said Hans. "If it's a girl, they'll name her Sarah, another Biblical name, but her middle name will be Phyllis," said his wife – to – be. "So, we're honored, either way," said Hans. "We'll probably be doing the same with our children, don't you think?" said Phyllis. "Oh, yes, our children..." said Hans, yes, we'll have to talk about that." "Talking isn't what gets it done," said Phyllis, "I've read a book about it on that subject." "Oh, you know what I mean," said Hans, "you are a tease, you know that? " Then, on impulse, Hans pulled the car over to the side of the street, and gave his Phyllis a teasing kiss, before continuing on to the house. Before they got there, Phyllis told Hans how she had been saving money to her savings account, for a car for them, so they wouldn't have to borrow a truck or a car, from Dan Blocker, or Father Jim, to get places. "I've saved enough to get a nice 1939 Chevrolet, selling for $158," said Phyllis. "How could you save that much?" said Hans. "From the 3rd week on I've been putting $25, then $10 a week until I had enough. I took it from the extra money from your pay, or from my pay," said Phyllis, "after I made a payment on the loan. Just think, only the two people who bought the last two 1942 cars here, & the mayor, who has a 1940 car, will have a newer car than ours. You'll do the driving, as you know how I am with that darned clutch." "Yes, I heard of when you drove your father's car, and some people had to come and work on it, to get it started," said Hans. "They said I stripped the gears, whatever that means," said Phyllis. "Well, I can teach you how to drive, so you can use it for a trip when I'm working," said Hans. "Just show me how to work that darned clutch," said Phyllis.

They came to the house, it didn't look any different from the outside. But as Hans opened the front door, he noticed the big, main room, and especially, the big table. "Where did that come from?" said Hans. "I bought it, and a lot of other things, with the extra money from your pay each week," said Phyllis. Then she told him of the silverware, dishes, cooking utensils, chairs, a small couch, a new mattress for the bed, and even an electric refrigerator. Then she took him upstairs and showed him the nice dresser she had someone make, like the one he gave to

Cora and Andrew. "I already have a few of my clothes in it," said Phyllis, "we can put the rest of our clothes in it just before we are married." "Speaking of marriage," said Hans, "we hadn't yet set a date, and then I had to go away for my assignment. How about 4 weeks from today, the last Saturday in June?" "Oh, I'd marry you tomorrow," said Phyllis. "That's sweet, but I know how you women like to take time for all of the planning, for the big day," said Hans. "All we have so far is our best man and maid of honor," said Phyllis, "Andrew and Cora Zerbee. "We'll get others for the rest of the wedding party," said Hans, "people from the Zerbees, the Blockers, & also the mayor's family. We'll have most of the people Cora and Andrew had for their own wedding. Four weeks is plenty of time for planning everything." Phyllis then looked up at Hans, and said: "I don't know if I can wait four weeks." Hans then gave her a nice, sweet kiss, and Phyllis said: "I can wait four weeks." So they left, with Hans giving Phyllis many compliments for what she had done with the house. "You told me to 'mind the store,'" said Phyllis. After dropping Phyllis off at her parent's house, he drove the car back to the rectory, and took the horse, for his ride back to the ranch.

Sunday Hans was welcomed back by all the choir members, and a few others after Mass. Then he went back to the ranch to do a few odd chores, to make up for the time he would be missing, the next morning. It seemed nice to do his old job, and not have to worry about someone knowing who he was, as he did in his last job, with the government.

Monday morning, after breakfast, Hans took Dan's truck, Dan was in the field with other workers, and didn't need it for now. He brought his check for $50 that the military had given him, for his week of training, and cashed it at the bank, then took out $129 of the $130 and change from his ring account, money he had earned as he did extra work for Dan Blocker, and others who needed help with something. Then he went to the jeweler, where he and Phyllis had looked at the diamond rings, mostly the smaller ones. But Hans had talked to the jeweler after, about the largest ring he had, to get for Phyllis, which was priced at

$179. "Hello, Mr. Kruber,' said the jeweler, as he saw Hans come in. "Please, it's Hans, we're friends," said Hans. "So, you're to get the ring you talked to me about?" said the jeweler. "Yes, I am," said Hans. "Well, I figured you would be back for it, but you can't have the ring you looked at," said the jeweler, "you see, after I talked with you I looked at the ring again, and realized it was not Phyllis' size, it was too small for her finger. But I had some sales of two small rings, a pearl necklace, and a bracelet, so I used the money to get another ring like the one you looked at, but in Phyllis' size. Some jewelers had a new gadget you can use, for making a ring a little larger, but I don't have one of those. The one you saw was 1.47 carats, the new one I got has 1.53 carats, a little bigger, but the price is the same. If you can put $85 down on it now, you can pay me the rest at $5 a week, if that's all right with you." As the jeweler was talking Hans took the money out of his pocket, and laid the $179 on top of the glass display case. The store owner looked at it, and then counted it quickly. "I don't know how you did it," said the store owner, "I'll get you a receipt. I'll also have a small ring box for it, for when you give it to Phyllis." As Hans took the ring, in its box, he told the store owner that he was invited to the wedding. "Thank you, that will be nice, my wife will be glad to hear about it," said the store owner. "Oh, bring her, too," said Hans, "I know women like weddings." "Yes, mine does, it's been three years since she last went to a wedding,' said the store owner. "You'll get an invitation in the mail," said Hans.

So Hans arranged to give Phyllis the ring by calling Andrew Zerbee at his father's house, as he asked if he could bring Phyllis to his house Friday, after he was through work. "Yes, bring Phyllis," said Andrew, "come at night, for supper, Cora will be glad to have you." "Thank you," said Hans, "just don't say anything to Phyllis." "Mum's the word," said Andrew.

After finishing with his work on the ranch, Hans washed up and changed into clean clothes. About 6 o'clock he borrowed Dan's truck, and drove to the Thaxter house. It was already about 6:20, & Phyllis kissed Hans, then asked him where they were going. "It's a surprise," said Hans, "I have something I want to ask you, after supper." As they rode along, soon Phyllis could see that they were going to the Zerbee farm. Hans drove the truck past the main house, and on to Andrew's and Cora's house. They were welcomed, and had a nice supper with Andrew and Cora. All during the meal Phyllis kept glancing at Hans, as she was thinking to herself, "what is my man up to?"

After a nice fish supper, with some macaroni & cheese, they all went to the living room, where Hans had Phyllis sit on the couch, as Andrew and Cora looked on. Hans got down on one knee, and said, "Will you marry me?" As Phyllis gave a surprised look, she said: "You already proposed to me." "Yes, but we were alone then, I wanted to ask you, with witnesses," said Hans, "so, what is your answer?" "What? Oh Hans, yes" said Phyllis, as she stood up and kissed Hans. Hans then had Phyllis sit back down on the couch, as he reached in his pocket, and brought out the ring box, which he opened in front of her. Phyllis' eyes opened wide as she saw the ring, as Hans took it from the box it was in. Phyllis mechanically held out her left hand, and Hans put the ring on her finger. "Hans!" said an excited woman, "that's not one of the ones we were looking at, the half carat ones." "I told you I was saving for your ring," said Hans. "This is the big one we glanced at," said Phyllis. "No, the one we glanced at wasn't your size, the jeweler got another one, this one is 1.53 carats. The jeweler says that he knows of only one woman in town with a larger one, the mayor's wife," said Hans. Cora then said, "It's bigger than my mom's ring." "Well, three weeks from tomorrow is the wedding, we will probably have most of the people you had, in our wedding party," said Hans, "with you two, of course, standing next to us at the altar."

Hans then took Phyllis to her home, and, after a few goodbye kisses, she left Hans, and went inside to show her ring to her parents. The next day she showed off her ring to her boss, and to some people that she knew who came to the diner. On Sunday she showed it to the choir, they all knew her, and to Father Jim and Marie. Everything was set now for Hans' and Phyllis' future, as they would be getting a car for their transportation, as the war went on, with the Allies preparing for the ending of the war, in Europe.

Hans looked forward to his life with Phyllis, but also looked back, to when his church was closed in Germany, his induction into the army, his training for being a spy, his capture and imprisonment, his escape, his own discovery of the fine country he was in, his coming back to his Church, his joining the choir, the jobs he worked, his meeting a girl he fell in love with, his becoming a citizen, the questioning he went through with the FBI, and his eventual service for his country. And in the next year the Allied forces would begin their liberation of Europe, and the next year, the surrender of Japan, so that the biggest and bloodiest conflict the world had ever seen would come to an end, thanks be to God.

AUTHOR'S NOTE

This story has a lot of truth in it, especially about the World War II history. In war there are always prisoners of war, who do their best to escape. When my father, Harry F. Ryniker, was in the army in 1942, he was stationed for a while in the camp in Oklahoma that I wrote about earlier in the story. Although it was early in the war for the U. S., there were more than 200 German prisoners of war there, and my father said that a few of them could speak English. Most German escapees would be apprehended before long, since they couldn't speak English, but the ones who could speak English could blend in with those in their part of the country, and eventually become Americanized, since they could see what a better way of life we had, compared to the way of life in Hitler's Germany. They would come to live a normal life, with a wife and children, in most cases. I suspect that there are a thousand or more Americans today who have no idea that their father, or grandfather, was a German POW. The German escapees appreciated this wonderful nation that we live in. It's a shame that many Americans today take our nation for granted, and don't think of the millions of people in the world who are not free.

www.ingramcontent.com/pod-product-compliance
Lightning Source LLC
Chambersburg PA
CBHW052113030426
42335CB00025B/2962